The ENGLISHMAN and DETROIT

The ENGLISHMAN and **DETROIT**

A British Entrepreneur
Helps Restore a City's Confidence

JOHN GALLAGHER

First Parafine Press Edition 2021
ISBN: 978-1-950843-38-1

Parafine Press
5322 Fleet Avenue, Cleveland, Ohio 44105
www.parafinepress.com
Book design by Meredith Pangrace
Cover design by David Wilson

To Sheu-Jane and to the memory of my parents

TABLE OF CONTENTS

PREFACE

If you want to start an argument in Detroit, tell longtime residents that their city is so broken that it has become a blank canvas that requires outsiders to come in to fix it.

With a touch of asperity, city dwellers will tell you that "Detroit never left." The city's population, though much reduced from its peak years, still roughly equals that of Cleveland and Pittsburgh combined. Detroit factories still churn out vehicles, the music scene remains as vibrant as ever, and the city's largely African American populace is anything but resigned to failure. Newcomers to the city, while welcome, need to remember that, and never ever say they came to Detroit to "save the city" from itself.

But acknowledging this much, also note that newcomers to Detroit have played crucial roles at every milepost of the city's 300-plus-year history. Detroit's greatest architect, Albert Kahn, immigrated to Detroit from Germany; the city's greatest labor leader, Walter Reuther, arrived from West Virginia; civil rights icon Rosa Parks did important work in Detroit after her more famous protest in Montgomery; the city's first African American mayor, Coleman Young, was born in Alabama. And, of course, there were the untold thousands of Appalachian whites and sharecropper Blacks who migrated to the city to work in the early auto factories. For nearly all its three centuries and more, Detroit created such a vortex of opportunity that it drew talented people from afar, women and men who devoted their lives to the city and who changed it for the better.

In that spirit, this book tells the story of another newcomer to Detroit and how he helped the city in the first two decades of the new century. This is the sort of history that usually doesn't make the history books. But it seems to me, as a journalist who has covered Detroit's revitalization efforts for more than thirty years, that this story is worth telling. Before memories fade and the details are lost, it's good to get this tale down.

Randal Charlton came to Detroit in 2000 at a time when both he and the city had hit rock bottom. A once-successful British entrepreneur in agricultural sciences, Charlton had seen his career implode in the nineties due to bad luck and his own mistakes. A quixotic attempt to run a Cajunthemed restaurant in Florida had flamed out, leaving Charlton broke and depressed. For years afterward, nothing he tried clicked.

Detroit, as we know, was sinking to new depths at that same time, still losing population and jobs, still sliding toward municipal bankruptcy. Detroit, the home of Motown music and the Ford Mustang and the modern American labor movement, the city that once reigned as the world's industrial powerhouse, the arsenal of democracy in World War II, stood now as the international system of Rust Belt ruin. For virtually every metric to measure cities by—crime, poverty, school test scores, unemployment—Detroit stood alone at the far end of the scale. And in almost every other city in America, hard-pressed civic leaders, dealing with their own problems, consoled themselves with the thought, "At least we're not Detroit."

But as the flicker of confidence all but extinguished in both, Charlton and Detroit found each other. When, through an unlikely journey, Charlton, by then sixty years of age, arrived in Detroit in 2000 to set up a new biosciences start-up in the cheapest modern lab space he could find in the nation, he was ready to put to use every lesson he had learned in a very long career.

And, crucially for Detroit, he understood he was building not just a single business but preaching an entrepreneurial movement in Detroit, in a city where entrepreneurs and start-ups were all but unknown when he arrived, so dependent was Detroit on the giant industrial enterprises that formed the city's economic base for a hundred years.

Entrepreneurship in Detroit, the movement that Randal Charlton would help build, would look much different than it did in the flashy unicorn start-ups of the Silicon Valley. In a city with the highest poverty rate in the nation, Charlton understood he was bringing the gospel of entrepreneurship to Detroit's forgotten people—to laid-off auto workers, to women and men of color who lacked MBAs or perhaps even a college degree, to middle-aged and older people forced by a broken economy into reinventing themselves.

Charlton was not alone in promoting entrepreneurship as a way back for Detroit. But he was among the very first, and he played a leading role, first at his own start-up firm, then as head of TechTown, the business incubator that he transformed from a nearly bankrupt failure to the city's hub of entrepreneurial vitality. Indeed, it's not too far to say that the economic rebirth of the city in the form of start-up companies—hundreds, or even thousands, of entrepreneurs launching their own business dreams in a city that learned to welcome and nourish them—goes back to the fall of 2000 when Randal Charlton, shaking off the despair of his lost decade, set up shop in Detroit. To understand what Charlton brought to that task, we'll have to trace his earlier career through its many ups and downs. But as I said, the tale is worth the telling. The habits of thought and ways of doing things that he brought to his work in Detroit grew over many years in places far from the Motor City.

A necessary word here about race. As longtime Detroiters know, far too many outsiders have credited white people with reinventing the city, ignoring the hundreds of thousands of African American residents and the pastors, small business owners, political leaders, and others who fought for their city decade after decade. Randal Charlton happens to be a white man, but he wasn't one of the come-lately suburbanites who moved downtown in recent years to take advantage of a downtown revival already well underway. British by birth, an entrepreneur who had traveled to dozens of countries around the globe in a long and varied career, Charlton arrived in Detroit in 2000 when he was already well into late middle age. And over the next dozen years, he joined with Detroiters who, whatever their race or background, Black and white and Hispanic and Middle Eastern and Asian, were emotionally in much the same place as himself—nearly broke, discouraged by years of failure, but willing to grasp what looked like one more shot at reinvention.

How Charlton as an individual succeeded is a story of recovery set within a larger tale of a new economy emerging in Detroit, which is itself part of a much larger narrative of Detroit's ongoing struggle. Every house in Detroit, every block, every storefront and church and factory, has its own story to tell. This is just one of them. Perhaps by focusing on Randal Charlton's story we can inspire others to tell their own tales of Detroit—the millions of stories the city offers, unique and fascinating.

CHAPTER 1:

THE MAKING OF AN ENTREPRENEUR

When Nazi bombs rained down on England's capital during the early years of World War II, Londoners responded by sending their treasures to the countryside for safekeeping—foremost among those treasures were London's children. Tens of thousands of British children were sent to live with strangers during the German blitz. Many went through official government relocation programs, others informally. Among the latter were the two-and-a-half-year-old Randal Charlton and his infant sister, Victoria. Their father was away, fighting with British General Bernard Montgomery against Erwin Rommel's Afrika Corps. One night during a German air raid, their mother, Lucy, took the children down to London's Underground—or Tube—the subway stations that doubled as bomb shelters, and when the all-clear sounded, she found their flat had been damaged by the bombs. That proved too much for a mother with small children. She gathered what she could of their possessions, bought one-way tickets to the end of the line, and embarked on the next train. Hours later, she got off near a village called Bridgerule in Devon in southwest England, nearly 200 miles from the bombing she had left behind in London. Kids in tow, Lucy stopped in a village shop run by a Miss Pratt to seek advice on somewhere to stay. Miss Pratt suggested the family walk up the hill to Churchtown Farm, where owners Robert and Lily Bowden welcomed the newcomers like family. The Bowdens, like many other English in the countryside, saw sheltering displaced Londoners, especially the children, as their patriotic duty.

Whatever horrors Londoners were facing in the war, a boy like Charlton in the war years found Churchtown Farm close to heaven. Churchtown in the early 1940s more closely resembled a farm out of a Jane Austen novel than one of today's huge mechanized agricultural operations. Cart horses still pulled heavy loads, cows were still milked by hand, and the hens roamed free and laid their eggs in hedges or wherever they could make a nest. Geese padded up and down, hissing at passersby. Sheep, cattle, and pigs all mingled together in a typical farm of the day. The boy Randal learned to hand milk cows, starting off with a sedate cow named Rydon, and he hung around with the farm workers hauling in wagonloads of corn in the fall and threshing and milling grain for the cattle. He learned the ways of the wild animals, too—the foxes, badgers, rabbits, and birds that inhabited the farm.

The menagerie included a large human cast as well. Besides the owners and their son, there were the farm laborers who slept on the premises and a woman who cooked for them, and there were the other London children and parents who had fled the capital; every farm was urged to make each spare room and attic available to refugees. There were even the German prisoners of war on loan from the local POW camp who dug ditches and drained marshes to increase the ground available for growing crops. Charlton became friends with one particular German prisoner named Gustave who looked after him. Charlton remembers riding with Gustave in a horse cart to take grain to the local miller to grind into animal feed.

As the blue-eyed, sandy-haired Randal grew older, he returned repeatedly to Churchtown for visits with those who became his lifelong friends. And he never lost his interest in animal husbandry. In his late teens, when the time came to choose a college to attend, he picked Wye College in Kent, in the North Downs area east of London, to study agriculture sciences.

Charlton's father and grandfather had been journalists, and naturally, in the way of youth, he determined *not* to be a journalist, but at school the instinct to write took over. He published a short story about a soccer-playing monk called "Why the Monk Was Sent Off" and was astonished to receive the sum of £10 for it. He kept the check on his wall for a long time before cashing it for beer money. After graduating, he got a reporting job with *Farmer's Weekly,* the largest agriculture publication in Britain.

Farmer's Weekly was a pretty conservative place in the late 1960s. Even after years, staffers would still address each other by their last names, as in "Mr. Charlton," and they communicated by sending memos in envelopes through the interoffice mail instead of just popping into a coworker's office for a chat. Young Randal got a reputation as a bit of an upstart. He was eager to write about all the new scientific breakthroughs that would soon revolutionize farming and animal care around the globe. And his natural instincts as a writer who wanted to be read led him to look for catchy ways to cover the somewhat dry material. He developed a style in which he wrote about the people as well as the technology. After all, he would say, when you get down to it, there were individuals who made the technology work because they were passionate about it. Within a year or so, he had won an award as the best agricultural journalist in Britain under the age of thirty, and then, in the same year, the award for best journalist in the open competition for all ages. The prize was a month's scholarship to study farming techniques in Sweden. It was a pretty lonely month for him, not speaking Swedish and trying to meet with farmers who mostly didn't speak English. Then he was back home and, with what he later realized was the entrepreneurial spark, he took a new job with a competing publication that had the bad luck to fold a month later.

So, award-winning but out of work, Charlton joined the Milk Marketing Board of England and Wales, the dairy cooperative for more than 100,000 farmers producing milk and dairy products. At that time, dairy farmers in Britain were just beginning to understand that they could greatly increase their milk production if they impregnated their cows with the best available bull semen, instead of just using an average stud bull from down the lane. Liquid nitrogen had just been found to perfectly freeze bull semen for shipment. The milk board had a "Better Breeding" program to sell this innovative technology to farmers, and as their marketing man, Charlton looked for ways to jazz up the pitch. He learned that certain stud bulls contributed to much higher milk production, so in the monthly newsletter, he started a "Top of the Pops" chart, listing which bulls were the highest rated of the week. It was just like the song charts, with particular bulls rising or falling in the rankings each week. And at the end of the year, Charlton reported that a bull with the fanciful name of Hunday Falcon V was the top stud bull in the land in terms of how much milk came from the cows impregnated with his semen. Charlton hired a theatrical crown and took a photo of the crown being placed on the bull's head by a young model and ran a story called "King of the Stud." The story went around the world and got a full page in the *Daily Mirror* in Britain. Through such antics, the milk board saw dramatic increases in revenue from its "Better Breeding" program. During his three years there, Charlton got a taste of what it takes to drive sales and interest—ideas that would turn out to be useful years later in Detroit.

One night after work, over beer with some mates, a friend teased him: "Charlton, you think you're so bloody clever, why don't you start your own business?" Maybe the beer had gotten the better of him, but Charlton accepted the dare on the spot, and even the next morning resolved to go through with it. So he quit his job with the milk board, remortgaged his home, pooled his savings with his friends, and started a firm called Universal

Livestock Services. The idea was to sell the best bull semen in the market, not just in Britain but around the world. Charlton knew a farmer could collect semen from a stud bull once or twice a week, and each collection, properly handled and diluted, could impregnate 500 or 600 cows. So one prize stud could make a dramatic impact on milk production around the world.

The partners looked at a map and tried to figure out where their services were most needed. They settled on Australia. So Charlton found himself Down Under, calling on farmers, trying to sell them on the need for their product. He found it tough going. The orders didn't come, and his little pot of cash was diminishing rapidly. Outback farmers are naturally conservative, and their attitude toward Brits was that they were all "pommy bastards," a playfully affectionate phase thought to be based on "Prisoner of Mother England" since Britain had populated Down Under with its transported criminals in colonial times. Charlton feared he wasn't making any headway. He learned how lonely life can be for what Americans now call a road warrior. But he learned some positive lessons, too. He contacted the British Embassy and got a wealth of leads. "You have no idea," he would say later, "how powerful an introduction it is to say on a sales call in a foreign land, 'I'm calling at the suggestion of the British Embassy.'" And he wrangled an interview on a radio talk show to talk about his work. He told the interviewer, who didn't know Charlton except as one of those pommy bastards, to throw everything he had at him as he explained his mission. The interview wasn't polite, but it had that spark, and he started to get a lot of leads, but orders still proved elusive. The problem was that Aussie farmers had their own milk board, which monopolized the provision of the sort of DNA material Charlton was marketing. And they had a thousand bulls to collect from while he and his mates had just six back in England. He went around from cattle ranches to dairy farms to cattle breeding centers, growing increasing lonely and disappointed.

He ended up feeling really sorry for himself in Melbourne. He had sworn he would not go back without an order, but he had reached the end of the line. He developed strep throat and was ready to pack it in and head home. But he had one more call scheduled at one last cattle breeding center called Victorian Artificial Breeders. It was the biggest organization in Australia, and he knew they were working with the monopoly milk marketing board. And he knew, as he put it, that there was as-close-to-zero-as-dammit-is-to-swearing-chance of getting an order.

But this was where he learned one of the great lessons of entrepreneurship—never give up. He was talking with the manager and telling him all about his firm, and the manager interrupted and asked, "How much have you got?" Charlton kept on with his spiel about the business and the manager interrupted again and said, "No, how much have you got?" Eventually, he all but shouted at Charlton: "Look, do you want to sell what you've got or not?" Charlton was stunned. He quickly worked out a price and the manager said, "I'll take it." Charlton was shocked into learning something, which is when the customer says "yes," you shut up and take the order. He later found that the manager had just that morning received word from the milk marketing board that one of the prize bulls that was supposed to supply semen for his orders was no longer available. So Charlton's firm filled the gap for him. Many times in later years, when he found selling difficult, he remembered the golden rule: the last call is the one where you get the order. He was able to go home to England with the order, and University Livestock Services was on its way.

Now, if the adventures of a homesick young Brit selling bull semen in Australia seem far removed from the concerns of Detroit, have patience. Randal Charlton was developing habits of thoughts and ways of doing things that would pay off thirty years later for the Motor City.

CHAPTER 2:
DETROIT'S FIRST ENTREPRENEURS

Detroit, too, had once welcomed entrepreneurs, but that was long ago, long before Randal Charlton was born. Let's take a moment to remember that time.

Historians of industry sometimes call Detroit the Silicon Valley of the early twentieth century. Just as the area around Palo Alto, California, welcomed the nascent computer industry and its collection of nerds, garage tinkerers, marketing geniuses, and venture investors in the decades after World War II, so too did mechanics, manufacturing gurus, and savvy investors flock to Detroit at the turn of the twentieth century and shortly after.

Detroit had to fight to become the home of the auto industry, because at first it appeared that New England might capture the industry. New England, with its "Connecticut Yankee" history of mills and manufacturing, did produce cars in those first hopeful years of the new century. But New Englanders were betting on the wrong propulsion technology—steam and electric batteries rather than gas-powered internal combustion engines. Colonel Albert Pope, one such New Englander who produced steamers, believed that nobody would want to sit atop an engine that harnessed gas vapor explosions. But early steam cars didn't produce the power needed, and electric batteries (as manufacturers rediscovered a century later) proved heavy, bulky, and in need of frequent recharging. One event of the day illustrated the dilemma facing the steam and battery champions. Dr. H. M. Jackson of Vermont and his chauffeur completed the first recorded coast-to-coast trip in a motorcar in 1903 powered by a gasoline engine. Battery charging would have been impractical in the West's wide-open spaces, and water holes were too far apart for the needs of steam.

Then, too, a happy accident of geography favored Detroit. Gasoline was then refined from petroleum fields in nearby Pennsylvania, Ohio, and Indiana—a short distance from Detroit. And Detroiters brought their own manufacturing expertise to the game, and it proved even a better match for the auto industry than the mills of New England. Detroit factories had produced railroad cars for many years, creating a class of workers skilled in wheels, axles, bodies, and the like. Easily available lumber from northern Michigan, the source of many forestry fortunes, had also made Detroit a center for the carriage industry, which produced skilled carpenters, upholsterers, leather workers, and more. These workers, too, could easily transfer their skills to the automotive shop floor.

And as a port city on the Great Lakes, Detroit had long operated dry docks where generations of mechanics learned the fine points of propulsive technology. Some of the men who later became the stuff of legend in the new auto industry—Henry Ford among them—brought years of expertise with marine engines to the task of mass-producing cars.

So with this critical mass of talent, manufacturing facilities, ambition, and money to invest from the lumber and railroad industries, Detroit grew its automotive industry at breakneck speed. Many of the entrepreneurs entering the industry simply switched from an earlier product to cars. A company called Peerless had first produced clothes wringers in the 1860s and then bicycles in the early 1890s; it was one of many who switched to making cars. The car known as the Rambler got its name from a bicycle by the same name when its manufacturer switched into autos. Companies producing everything from birdcages to sewing machines converted to automotive manufacturing. In 1900, there were seventy-two US companies making motorcars; another 138 companies joined them over the next three years.

And there were fortunes to be made. In those early years, before his own name got attached to a vehicle, Walter Chrysler brought his manufacturing skill to the task of revamping the production line at Buick. He soon tripled production. Hired in at $6,000 a year, within several years, he was president of Buick at a salary of $500,000 a year.

It was a heady time, a revolutionary time. And like so many revolutionary moments, when anything and everything seemed possible, it passed all too quickly. The nation's demand for cars proved so enormous that it required manufacturing on a vast scale. The American motorcar would not become, as some in those early years believed, a luxury item for doctors, lawyers, bankers, and others of substantial means. Henry Ford preached that the motorcar had to become a peoples' car; he would mass-produce autos in numbers unimaginable in those first early years of handcrafted engines and bodies.

In this new industry, demand for labor would spur one of the great mass migrations in American history. Poor Appalachian whites and sharecropper Blacks moved north to work for the likes of Ford, joining untold thousands of immigrants from overseas. The tool shops and workhouses of the nineteenth century morphed into the gargantuan factories of the future, led first by Ford's Highland Park plant, where the population of that tiny village grew from 400 in 1900 to 40,000 in 1920. The gigantic River Rouge plant near Detroit opened in 1918, the greatest factory of its day, with a workforce of 100,000 and where crossed conveyor lines and smokestacks fired the imagination of artists and photographers. Vast quantities of steel, glass, rubber, and other materials poured in one end of these factories and finished automobiles rolled out the other.

Organizing this vast manufacturing enterprise became the task of professional managers. The entrepreneurs fell out of favor. The number of smaller car companies fell dramatically as those firms were gobbled up or driven out by those more successful. Company managers now were hard men who judged success by the unforgiving metrics of production and profit. In a remarkably short span of years, the Motor City had changed from a haven for entrepreneurs into the domain of the organization man, the corporate insider, the boss.

CHAPTER 3:

SHEIKS AND OTHER ADVENTURES

Randal Charlton and his partners at Universal Livestock Services enjoyed success over several years. They were running an expensive high-end business, importing bulls from the best European herds, bulls worth thousands of British pounds, into England. They were selling to beef ranchers and dairy farmers in Australia, Canada, and the United States, introducing major European breeds into those markets for the first time, breeds like the Friesian and Jersey from England, the Normande from France, the Dutch Friesian from the Netherlands, and the Chianina, Marchigiana, Romagnola, and Piemontese from Italy, among others.

They hit a snag in the 1970s when the OPEC oil embargo slammed the brakes on Western economies. Suddenly their customers couldn't take delivery of their expensive genetic material; the economy was just too uncertain for them to commit to an expensive order. So Charlton volunteered to explore whatever new markets might exist in North Africa and the Middle East. A few days later, he was flying into Libya aboard a Libyan passenger jet that the pilot flew like a fighter plane, scaring him half to death. Having landed in Tripoli, Charlton remembered his lessons and went to talk to the commercial officer at the British Embassy, who introduced him to the British ambassador, who happened to know the Libyan agriculture minister. So Charlton went back to his hotel and called the government offices and gradually made his way up the chain, using his line, "I'm calling at the suggestion of the British ambassador." And he got an interview for the next day.

The Libyans, he learned, were extremely interested in increasing their beef and milk production, but they didn't want the costly genetic material that Charlton's firm offered. Instead, Libyan agriculture was in such a primitive state that they wanted the very basics—milking machines, ear tags for cows, irrigation equipment, sheepshearing tools, animal feeders, proper animal housing, veterinary supplies, the works. What they wanted was a lot of the simple stuff that the British kept in their farm museums back in England.

So Charlton took the order and went home and told his partners that the Libyans wanted a turnkey operation. They may have wanted some great cows, but they wanted the farm to go with them—the fences, irrigation, everything—and they wanted Charlton to go there and stay for a year to run the farm and train locals to take it over. So Charlton came up with the name Farm Key, and that's how Universal Livestock Services pivoted into a new line of business. Over the next sixteen years, Charlton traveled throughout the Middle East, setting up cattle and dairy farms in Lebanon, Libya, Egypt, Morocco, Algeria, Saudi Arabia—all the Arab nations. He had dinner with the king of Saudi Arabia and royalty in Jordan.

Once, he flew thirty-six pregnant Jersey cows and one rambunctious Jersey bull into a desert landing strip in northern Saudi Arabia for a sheik who was hoping to build up his dairy herd. The contract called for Charlton to merely deliver the cattle, but upon arrival, he saw that the sheik's existing herd suffered many ailments. Many of the 1,000 or so cattle there were sick or dying. Cattle weren't getting enough water and their diet was out of balance; many were suffering from standing in the hot sun during the heat of the day. So instead of just delivering their cattle and flying back to England, Charlton stayed for a few weeks to help the sheik as best he could. Each night, he dined late in the sheik's guesthouse, sitting cross-legged on the floor and eating dinner with his right hand from a common platter piled high with rice and meat. Finally, with trust established after many such dinners, the sheik asked Charlton if he could manage the entire herd for him. In a few weeks, Charlton had dozens of skilled agricultural workers in the desert, and soon they had doubled and then tripled the herd's milk production.

By around 1980, when Charlton was nearing forty, he'd done business of one sort or another in about forty countries. When arriving in a new country, even driving on the way in from the airport to his hotel, he would see things that would be business opportunities. "Every country has its own gaps in the marketplace," he would say. He found the life incredibly stimulating.

Charlton happened to have a gall bladder operation about that time, and when he came back to the office, he and his partners discussed what to do next. His partners suggested that he go to America for a few weeks to scout opportunities in the life sciences there. This was no hardship for him; Charlton was the sort of Englishman who fell in love with America in his youth. In college in Britain in 1960, he had listened to John F. Kennedy's campaign speeches in his dorm room. Charlton had been fascinated with the American way of life and Americans' willingness to try anything, to jump in.

He flew to Washington, DC, and spent a couple of weeks in a Holiday Inn. The aftereffects of his gall bladder surgery still wore on him; he would work in the mornings, be exhausted by lunchtime, and rest in the afternoon. But he hooked up with the Biotech Industry Association, then a new group, and he spent two weeks there researching the field and then flew around the country calling on people, looking for technology partners. He went to San Francisco, New York City, up to Connecticut. In Hartford, he happened to meet Dr. Alan Walton, a scientist and investor in new technology who had a company called University Genetics that was doing work in human genetics, but was thinking of getting into animal genetics; it was already NASDAQ-listed. As they chatted, Walton warmed to Charlton immediately, to his sunny personality and openness to new ideas. "I must say that when he came to visit us I immediately—I don't want this misinterpreted—sort of fell in love with him," Walton said much later. "He's such a wonderful character. Being a Brit myself I suppose I immediately trust that he was a person I could work with." Walton asked him where he was flying to next; Charlton told him Boston for the Biotech Industry Association conference. A day or two later, Charlton was eating breakfast at the Copley Plaza in Boston when in walked Alan Walton. He had driven four hours up to see Charlton. "I hadn't expected to see him again so soon after our lunch the previous day," Charlton said much later. "He said he'd been thinking all night about our conversation."

As Walton said later, "I was faced with a problem most biotech CEOs are faced with, and that is if you start a company and its drug-related, it's going to take you fifteen years and several hundred million dollars to get a drug. I had to find a method somehow or other of generating revenues in the first, second, or third year of operations, which is pretty difficult." But as he and Charlton talked, the idea emerged that if they could utilize embryos from top-line animals, Holsteins for example, and could sell them internationally to countries such as Indonesia, where they have very inferior cattle, this could be an almost instantaneous source of revenue. "And to put some numbers on this," Walton said, "good Holsteins were probably worth about $4,000 each in this country, and an Indonesia yak a couple of hundred dollars. So if you could implant the embryo in the yak and give birth to a Holstein you would have obviously generated an animal worth many times what its parent was. And it cost about $400 to produce an embryo at the time. And I think the rate of success of freezing an embryo from a Holstein in this country and taking it somewhere else in the world was about a 50 percent success rate. We laughingly say in the first-class seat on a plane you could take a whole herd of cows. So the economics looked very good."

This wasn't very long after the first successful transspecies embryo transfer was performed, at the Bronx Zoo, where they had successfully bred an Indian gaur by implanting an embryo in a Holstein cow, so the Holstein cow had given birth to an Indian bison, which was pretty clever. So this looked like a feasible way of going about things. And, having hit it off on a personal basis and sharing an interest in the emerging technology, Walton thought that Charlton would be the guy to take on the task for him.

At first Charlton had demurred; he was returning to England shortly. But Walton persisted, and he suggested Charlton talk to his partners back home about extending his time in the United States. So Charlton flew home to England, found his partners were open to the idea, and flew back to the United States, setting up in Hartford to start running Alan Walton's small but promising company. At that time, it was much easier for a Brit, particularly one with some qualifications, to get to the States than it would be decades later when homeland security became such a big concern. So they decided to join forces. "Basically, he came to work for University Genetics and ran the animal reproduction division, animal cloning division," Walton said.

First, Charlton started developing a company called American Diagnostic Sales as a subsidiary, working on pregnancy tests for cows. After about a year, Walton told him that he was getting out of managing start-ups; Walton saw himself as a researcher and an investor. He was eager to launch a new investment firm called Oxford Venture Partners, which subsequently did quite well. (We'll return to Oxford and Walton again later in this book.) So Charlton took over as chairman and CEO of University Genetics. For a few years, he had five subsidiary companies doing all sorts of interesting stuff—artificial insemination of cows, embryo transfer, pregnancy testing. He had a firm called Agrogene that was cloning plants. He signed a contract with Dole Food Company to make banana trees more resistant to disease. None of these subsidiaries was showing a profit yet, but most were starting to take in revenue, so it was promising. This was all incredibly exciting for Charlton, both the technology and the challenge of commercializing all the research coming out of universities. About this time, he got his permanent residency card in the United States.

Years later, Charlton would recall this as a pretty idyllic period in his life. He immensely enjoyed the American scene, and his company was doing exciting things. One of his board members was Orville Freeman, who had served as President John F. Kennedy's secretary of agriculture, and Charlton found him a delightful mentor. The field of biotechnology was growing very quickly. The future stretched out before him.

Then, on Monday, October 19, 1987, Charlton was sitting in his office in Connecticut overlooking the Saugatuck River, having a phone conversation with an investment group on Long Island, New York, who were about to lend him $3 million in financing on top of the $300,000 they'd already advanced. Outside his window, Charlton could see the autumn leaves silently floating down to land in the river, and he remembers thinking that life was as close to perfect as it ever could be.

Then the investor on the phone said, "Wait a moment. There's something happening on Wall Street."

CHAPTER 4:
THE GREAT CRASH

By now, well into the twenty-first century, investors have lived through enough crashes of the stock market, including the meltdown in the financial markets that triggered the Great Recession of 2007–09, that they no longer get too jumpy about a market correction. But the crash of October 1987 rocked Wall Street like nothing since the Great Depression of 1929. There were several reasons for the crash. The bull market had been running for several years; inflation was beginning to rise; earnings estimates were trending lower even as market valuations remained high. Investors also believed that portfolio insurance would soften the blow of losses, but in fact, it mostly encouraged excessive risk-taking. All those contributed as prices began to wobble and then drop, but the magnitude of the crash stemmed from another reason: big investment houses had come to rely on the relatively new computerized trading programs, which supposedly insured against excessive losses by automatically dumping shares at certain trigger points as the price declined. A sensible precaution for individual firms, nobody seemed to understand what would happen when everyone was using those programs at the same time, and since the same programs also limited buying, there were no buyers willing to look for now underpriced stocks as the market nose-dived. Liquidity disappeared just as it was needed most. The trading programs kept driving down prices in a vain attempt to find buyers; stock prices, even for the most highly rated companies, just kept falling. When October 19 ended, the Dow Jones Industrial Average had tanked 22 percent—the biggest one-day drop in its history.

Stocks eventually recovered, of course. The market today is many times higher than before the 1987 crash, and the economy has soldiered through its ups and downs, including the most recent crash during 2020's coronavirus crisis. Investors no longer scare quite so easily. But the 1987 crash threw a nasty fright into investors of the day. That explains in large measure what happened to Charlton in the aftermath.

The investor had said, "There's something happening on Wall Street. Hang on." And he left Charlton on hold for a minute or two. When he came back, he hurriedly broke off the call, saying he'd call back. Charlton switched on the TV news, thinking the trouble couldn't be that bad, but of course it was even worse.

A week went by. Then the calls and letters from the investors' attorney started; they were cancelling the $3 million investment and demanding the $300,000 back. Charlton told them he couldn't give it to them; he had already used it. The investors took him to federal court in Bridgeport. Charlton remembers seeing the helicopters flying in with the hotshot lawyers for the investors. But the federal judge, after hearing all sides, said he found Charlton a good and credible witness, and his recommendation was that the sides work something out. The deal was that Charlton's firm could keep the $300,000, but the $3 million commitment was voided. That more or less spelled the end of University Genetics, although Charlton didn't know it at the time. He was advised by more than one person to put the company in Chapter 11, but Charlton, being British, just couldn't get his mind around the American willingness to declare bankruptcy. He came from a culture where bankruptcy was almost as big a crime as theft. When you went into court, if you were declared bankrupt, you had to empty your pockets and take off your watch before leaving the court, and it was the end of your career, really. It was a different attitude than in the United States, where failure was tolerated; it certainly wasn't tolerated in the United Kingdom. Charlton spent the next four years paying off the creditors of University Genetics. He paid off everyone by gradually selling off the assets of the firm. It was probably one of the hardest periods of his life. For several months he tried to raise cash from other sources before realizing that the investors just weren't there. His days became consumed with rounds of shareholders and creditors screaming down the phone line, and meetings and court hearings that any entrepreneur in that situation knows all too well.

Eventually, Charlton was left with just one subsidiary, Agrogene, which had a five-acre research facility in Lake Worth, Florida. He knew he could no longer keep up an expensive corporate office in Westport, Connecticut, so he moved the company down to Florida. There he had extensive greenhouses and other facilities, and the site was doing applied research for Dole and a couple of other firms, as well as growing miniature roses for the Mother's Day market. The firm had some limited success, but not enough. The final straw was when their batch of roses—which must mature to perfection right for Mother's Day—weren't ready in time. So Charlton sold off all the remaining assets, trying to pay down the $4 million debt to creditors. Everybody got something, although not everyone got 100 cents on the dollar. People would call him each week, demanding their money, and he would say, "Look, I'm writing checks today to anyone willing to take fifty cents on the dollar. I can give you that or you can wait until next week." Eventually, everyone got something, and Charlton was left with a shell public company with no assets.

Then entered Bill Straughan of Houston, Texas, who some thought to be the illegitimate son of politician Huey Long. He was a very wealthy guy involved in a whole bunch of businesses—insurance, waste disposal, and more—and he was interested in buying a shell public company for his own reasons. He bought the company and asked Charlton to move to Texas for a few months with all the documentation, shareholder records, and so forth. So Charlton decamped to Houston temporarily to work with him. One morning, Straughan said, "Charlton, I think we're done," so Charlton hired a car and drove back home to Sarasota, Florida, where he had moved for business.

It was time to start over yet again. Charlton had turned fifty not long before. The previous twenty-five years had flown by. By now he was no longer the cocky young public relations whiz at the milk board, the guy who had bantered with sheiks in a desert tent. But, though he was out of work now, he thought he had a lot to show for it all. He'd been in business for going on thirty years, he'd run multiple public companies, traveled all over the world, made a fair amount of money, had his winners and losers. Now, for the first time in decades, he had time on his hands and no clear idea of what he was going to do. That was important for what came next.

On the way back to Florida, he wanted to stop in to see something of Cajun country. With his love for America, he had developed a fascination with the whole New Orleans mystique; he had read a biography of Huey Long entitled *Louisiana Hayride*, and he thought he just needed to take a look at this state because it seemed so different from the rest of America. He stopped in Baton Rouge, was not impressed with the rather Germanic look of the government buildings in the state capital, but then toured around New Orleans and the bayou region. "To say I fell in love was an understatement," he said much later. "I can see now that I had been at loose ends, and I fell a little too hard and fast for the culture. I assure you I wasn't drinking when I decided, 'My God, I've got to take New Orleans back to Florida with me.'"

CHAPTER 5:

DETROIT TO ENTREPRENEURS: "CRAP!"

The sort of entrepreneur that Randal Charlton was then—nimble, quick to spot and take advantage of new opportunities, unafraid of the challenges facing a new business—faced significant challenges in Detroit at the midpoint of the twentieth century. With its gigantic industrial enterprises, Detroit at midcentury might be said to be the most powerful business center in the nation. But the vast corporate organizations and the robust government planning operations that catered to them often crowded out the city's entrepreneurial culture. Indeed, the years on either side of the century's midpoint would prove ruinous for many entrepreneurs in Detroit, none more so than the African American business owners in Detroit's famed Black Bottom district.

Located on the east side of downtown Detroit, Black Bottom was named for the rich dark soil that French explorers first found there. Black Bottom in the 1940s and 1950s housed the city's African American entrepreneurial class, with many thriving Black-owned businesses and the Paradise Valley entertainment zone, where Duke Ellington, Ella Fitzgerald, and Count Basie performed.

But in common with city planners elsewhere, Detroit's builders were enamored of building the new high-speed expressways that would reshape American life. Over numerous protests and with little or no regard for the African American businesses being destroyed, builders of the I-75 and I-375 freeways plowed multilane highways right through Hastings Street, the commercial heart of Black Bottom. Upscale residential projects such as Lafayette Park and the public housing projects to the north destroyed the rest in the name of progress.

In 2013, for a story for the *Detroit Free Press*, I spoke with Sidney Barthwell Jr., a Thirty-Sixth District Court magistrate whose father, Sidney Barthwell, ran a chain of pharmacies and ice cream shops in Black Bottom.

The sting of losing all the Black-owned entrepreneurial businesses in the district still rankled him all those decades later.

"Black Bottom, Paradise Valley, was indeed a paradise for Black entrepreneurial businesses," Barthwell told me. "Funeral homes, doctors—there were a dozen different Black-owned hospitals (in Black Bottom), because in those days, they wouldn't admit you into the major hospitals if you were African American. The Detroit Black community in its heyday was absolutely fantastic. It was better than Harlem."

The freeway builders and urban renewal planners did their work with the best of intentions. They believed they were scrubbing away deteriorating districts and building a healthier new city. But those good intentions meant little to the families displaced for freeways and other development, Barthwell said.

"That really just ripped the guts out of that neighborhood," he said. "It, in essence, destroyed my father's business. Basically, everybody had to move out. It was devastating, and it's never been the same again. Kind of like a Black diaspora. We went all over, where we could get in."

Something similar was taking place on the west side of downtown Detroit in the city's historic Corktown neighborhood. Initially settled by Irish immigrants in the nineteenth century, by the 1950s Corktown was heavily populated by Maltese immigrants. Construction of another expressway, the Lodge, demolished a good portion of the district, and the city's urban renewal plans tore down more of Corktown's historic blocks to build a light industrial park that turned out to be all but devoid of street life.

In the blocks north of downtown Detroit, still more homes and shops and businesses were razed to make way for an expanding hospital and university district.

Against the twin juggernauts of expressway building and urban renewal, the entrepreneurs of Corktown and Black Bottom, immigrants and people of color, stood not a chance.

Yet it was not only the entrepreneurs of color and immigrants that lost out in Detroit's love affair with bigness and industrial might. Two famous examples illustrate vividly how Detroit's mighty industrial giants were not ready to be challenged by new ways of doing things, no matter how creative the newcomers might be.

Preston Tucker saw his first motorcar at the age of six. That was in 1909, and if he remembered it more vividly than other childhood memories, that's because the sight of that shiny red car set him on his life's journey.

Born near Port Huron, about fifty miles northeast of Detroit along the shores of Lake Huron, Preston Tucker lost his father in infancy. His mother took him as a boy up to visit his grandfather in northern Michigan. It was the sort of country captured in Ernest Hemingway's first short stories—little villages set amid farmlands and forest, the towns centered on the sawmills that by this time were shutting down as the loggers went elsewhere to find new timberland. One summer day, the grandfather and grandson were clip-clopping along a dusty country road in their buggy behind a team of horses when they saw and heard an automobile approaching. Motorcars were just coming into their own then and the boy had never seen one other than in magazines. His grandfather alighted from the buggy, moved to the front of the team, and held the reins tightly so the horses wouldn't panic at the sound of the engine and the smell of the gasoline. The driver of the car, a local doctor, stopped and waved to the grandfather to walk the horses past him. Once safely past, the grandfather tied up the team and stopped to chat with the doctor. Young Preston drank in the sight of the car; he never remembered being so struck by anything so beautiful. And, as he said later, he never forgot it.

Preston Tucker proved a good son to his mother, seldom getting in trouble except that he always came home with his clothes full of dirt and grease from hanging out in garages and car lots. By the age of nineteen, he had joined the police department in the Detroit suburb of Lincoln Park. It was not because he cared much for law enforcement, but because he wanted to drive the squad cars—and motorcycles, too, in the nice weather—around town. He was a tinkerer from the beginning; one winter he borrowed an acetylene torch to cut a hole in the dash of a squad car so the heat from the engine would warm the unheated interiors. The dressing down he received hastened his departure from a career with the police.

He sold cars, ran a filling station, fell in love with auto racing, and took to visiting Indianapolis each May for the mighty 500-mile auto race. He loved speed. In one early job as an office boy at Chrysler, he wore roller skates in the office to make his deliveries faster. Coming around the corner one day, he collided with his boss; he left Chrysler shortly after that. And at the Indianapolis speedway, and in numerous garages and car lots, he learned the finer points of engine design, gas and oil consumption, tire wear, engine temperature, superchargers and disc brakes and downdraft carburetors, and everything else. One day, Tucker and a partner were driving with their wives to Indianapolis for the race when the radio broke.

To their wives' exasperation, the two men took the radio apart, spread all the parts on the hood of the car, and spent half the afternoon putting it back together. But it worked again once reassembled.

He had grown to six feet tall and was well-built, given to bow ties to go with his suits; the sort of man that many women found handsome. And he was good at his career. By his thirties, Tucker enjoyed a growing reputation as a leading promotor and salesman of cars. By 1935, he was building racing cars and marine engines, including racing cars for Henry Ford with high-powered V-8 engines. As the world charged toward global war, Tucker got an idea to sell combat vehicles to the military. He designed a high-speed armored car (in one test, it reportedly it hit 117 miles an hour) with a motorized gun turret on top. The military saw no need for the car itself but wanted the gun turret. Unfortunately, the government also seized Tucker's patent rights and royalties, so he never made anything from the widely used design.

Marine engines, aircraft engines, car parts—these seemed to be Preston Tucker's primary line in the early 1940s at his operation in Ypsilanti, outside Detroit. But inevitably, he dreamed of the new automobile he would build for the American people once the war ended. It would be fast, as powerful as any production car on the market, and it would include all the most innovative technology, advances that Detroit wouldn't adopt for years—an aluminum engine adopted from aircraft, an automatic transmission, an engine mounted in the rear, seats that swiveled for easy entry, headlights that rotated as a car went around a curve at night, a padded dash for safety, and so much more. By the time World War II ended in the summer of 1945, Tucker already had begun to assemble the team of engineers and finance guys who would create the car with him.

Whatever his faults as a corporate leader, as a showman and promotor Tucker was unexcelled. One associate said of him, "When he turns those big brown eyes on you, you'd better watch out!" He was not exactly a polished speaker, but he had the common touch that ordinary folk responded to. His marketing rallies proved wild affairs; people sent him fan mail, and some sent small contributions to help his enterprise.

At first, he called his concept the Tucker Torpedo to emphasize the vehicle's speed, but later abandoned that to stress safety. The model became the Tucker 48, named after the year of its introduction. His shop engineers and fans preferred the term Tin Goose, a term also applied to the Ford Trimotor aircraft when it was first introduced.

So here was the challenge to Detroit: Could a relatively unknown entrepreneur with a good idea but not much money break into the auto industry? The timing was certainly right. At America's entry into World War II, there were twenty-nine million vehicles on US roads; by war's end in 1945, there were just twenty-two million of those left, and even by the most generous estimate, most were clunkers. Detroit's Big Three—General Motors, Ford, and Chrysler—owned 90 percent of the car-producing market, and they couldn't wait to dump their wartime production of airplanes and tanks to return to selling cars to consumers. A golden era for sellers loomed. It might not last long, but for a few years at least, auto producers would be selling cars as fast as they could roll them off the assembly lines. A new guy with a good product and enough cash might just break in.

Into this market Preston Tucker strode as a man with a great concept but a weak bank account. One of the Tucker men, Charles Pearson, a former auto journalist who joined Tucker's public relations team, later wrote a memoir of those wild few years in the late forties. On almost every page, Pearson describes the shoestring operation in Tucker's factory in Chicago (where he moved because of difficulties getting space in Detroit). In a most telling incident, Pearson describes how engineers needed to heat test their new aluminum engine; lacking the million-dollar equipment the Big Three used in their factories, the engineers stuffed the prototype engine into the oven of Mrs. Tucker's kitchen at the Tucker house in Ypsilanti. They then assembled the parts on her kitchen floor, threw the finished engine in the back of a truck, and drove it to the factory in Chicago, leaving Mrs. Tucker with a ruined stove.

There was never enough money. Tucker's engineers wore their coats inside during winter because their design studio was unheated. *Automotive Industries* magazine reported that the smaller car producer Nash would spend $15 million on model changeovers and that Chrysler reportedly planned to spend $75 million on their new models—staggering sums to Tucker but normal business in Detroit. Tucker and his finance team tried innovative ways to raise cash; they sold franchises to potential dealers and raised several million dollars that way; a stock sale in the new Tucker corporation brought in $15 million; they even sold accessories that would go in future cars to buyers eagerly waiting for a Tucker 48. All that helped, and Tucker soon had more than two thousand workers toiling in his factory, testing concepts, machining parts, and hand-building the first few models.

But Tucker's creativity in raising money proved his downfall. The US Securities and Exchange Commission (SEC), the federal watchdog over the stock market, began to investigate whether Preston Tucker was really building a car or just raising cash for his own ends. It was widely believed that the Detroit auto elite and their allies in Congress were egging on the SEC, hoping to get rid of the upstart. The headlines about an SEC investigation hurt Tucker; when the SEC actually brought an indictment for fraud against him and several of his executives, his factory—stuffed with auto parts and half-finished vehicles—shut down. The government's case proved ridiculously weak, and the jury quickly found Tucker and his codefendants not guilty. But the damage had been done.

Only fifty-one Tucker 48s were finished, but those few cars, sleek and aerodynamic, quickly became the stuff of legend. An auto writer named Tom McCahill test drove one and told his readers in *Mechanix Illustrated* magazine: "This car is real dynamite! I accelerated from a dead standstill to 60 miles an hour in 10 seconds. Then I saw an open stretch of road ahead, so I opened the throttle wide. In no time at all, it seemed, we were doing 90 on the clock, 95, 100 and then 105—miles an hour, that is! This was the quickest 105 miles an hour I have ever reached. . . . The car is roomy and comfortable. It steers and handles better than any American car I have driven. As to roadability, it's in a class by itself. I'll really go out on a limb and say that if this car will stand up and prove reliable, it will make every other car made in America look like Harrigan's hack with the wheels off." But by then it was too late.

Preston Tucker never gave up his dream of building a new car. In the early 1950s, he was exploring the possibilities of raising money in Brazil, but it came to nothing. Suffering from lung cancer, Tucker died in 1956 at the age of fifty-three, a footnote in the annals of the Motor City.

If a cash-short visionary like Preston Tucker couldn't make it as an entrepreneur in Detroit, how about one of the nation's most famous industrialists?

Henry Kaiser, like Tucker, was born into the working class, his father a German immigrant shoemaker in upstate New York. As a teen, he earned cash as a photographer's apprentice, moved west to the state of Washington, sold hardware, got married, and rolled his savings into a small construction company. Fulfilling government construction contracts, Kaiser built a name for himself first in sand and gravel. During the Great Depression, he played major roles in building the government's monumental dam projects—the Boulder Dam, the Grand Coulee, the Bonneville. Already rich by the time of the Pearl Harbor attack in 1941,

Kaiser opened shipyards, supplied his own steel, and launched hundreds of Liberty and Victory ships for the US government during the war—cargo vessels needed to ferry vast amounts of food and war material for the two-ocean war. Speed became a fetish among his team; his son, Edgar, in charge of one shipbuilding line, got his men to produce a boat in a mere ten days. Then Clay Bedford, Kaiser's top production hand, got his men to build one is just four days; Edgar upped the ante and completed one in two days and a few hours. The Kaiser name began to attain an aura of miracle worker.

By the end of the war, Henry Kaiser was a national hero, his reputation akin to that of Henry Ford a couple of generations before him—a man who could rewrite the rules of industry to accomplish feats of production previously unknown. So when, as a sideline during the war, Kaiser got interested in cars, the public noticed. In 1942 he started buying up all kinds of cars and having his engineers break them down and reassemble them in novel ways to understand the possibilities. As World War II drew to its end, Kaiser signaled that he was serious: he envisioned a $400 peoples' car for the masses that would roll off the assembly lines in the millions, teaching the old guys in Detroit a lesson or two about new materials and new methods honed in sunny California.

There seemed no better time to try it. Like Preston Tucker, Henry Kaiser saw the vast opportunity in the nation's hunger for new cars. A golden time for auto companies was about to begin. Even at full production, Detroit would need a couple of years to fill the suppressed demand. And Kaiser saw reason for optimism everywhere. Of the $43 billion worth of war bonds outstanding, he said, "That's not debt. That's $43 billion in pure venture capital."

Then, too, the United Auto Workers (UAW) union was eager to see wartime production return as quickly as possible to civilian cars and trucks to keep its union members working. The UAW was happy to work with Kaiser, who offered them a deal that included incentive pay based on the number of cars produced.

So into this golden market strode possibly the most optimistic man in American industry. Physically, he may have appeared rumpled; in the words of a *Fortune* magazine writer in early 1946, "It would not be surprising if a little gravel rolled out of his trouser cuff." And *Fortune* went on, "Henry looks like the kind of Methodist deacon who keeps his mind on the service. . . . He never seems far from tears. About him there is a massive sentimentality. His speeches are almost maudlin, sprinkled with hallelujahs and Fourth of July oratory. He is so monumentally, so awe-inspiringly corny in his utterances that some sophisticates entirely miss the important thing—his dead-earnestness, which saves his speeches somehow." And the public loved it.

In July 1945, with Germany defeated and Japan less than a month away from the atomic bombing of Hiroshima and Nagasaki that would end the war, Kaiser partnered up with a man named Joe Frazer, himself almost a legend in the auto industry.

Frazer started his work life in overalls as an unskilled mechanic at the old Packard Plant on Detroit's east side in 1912. But that was just to get his hands dirty. He attended Yale, turned quickly to marketing cars, and prospered through fifteen years as general sales manager for Chrysler. At Willys-Overland, the maker of the Jeep, sales under Joe went from $9 million pre-Jeep to $170 million.

Kaiser and Frazer teamed up to produce a new kind of car—cheaper, made with innovative designs, something to bust up the Detroit monopoly. It would be daunting, sure; General Motors, Ford, and Chrysler owned 90 percent of the American car market, and a handful of other producers—Studebaker, Nash, Willys-Overland, and a few others—fought for the remaining scraps. But as Henry told Frazer early on, "All my life I've been going against the wind."

From the beginning, though, that Detroit monopoly looked down on the upstarts.

"I'll never forget," one rival auto executive said, "in the lobby of the Fairmont Hotel in San Francisco back in '45, the day Henry pulled out of his pocket a blank sheet of paper and drew, on the coffee table, the lines of a car. 'Now Joe,'" he said to Frazer, "'don't you think that would be perfectly wonderful?' Well of course the answer was that it wasn't wonderful or practical and that it was pure humbug."

This Detroit skepticism toward the newcomers ran deep. One Detroit executive said of Frazer: "Frazer never made a car in his life. All he did was sell them." Another exec said that Kaiser "hasn't found out yet that automobiles don't have bows, sterns, and rudders . . . they got the wrong name for the outfit. They ought to call it Barnum and Bailey." And among the quips circulating in Detroit was the story of a shipbuilder whom Henry Kaiser summoned eastward to Detroit. When this new guy first saw a Kaiser car, which carried its spare tire on the left, he fumed, "That's all wrong. You've got the life preserver on the port instead of the starboard side!" Sallies such as this were popular in the Motor City.

Kaiser was not deterred. "They ask me where we're going to get steel, how we're going to produce motors. Well, I'll tell you. The only thing that will limit our production will be our floor space. They tell me I'm going out on a limb. Well, that's where I like to be—way out on a limb. I like to be not afraid. We're out to service the nation, the whole world. We're out to produce thirteen million cars. If we don't, we'll get darn near it."

The public—and investors—surged to his side. In those early days, before producing a single car, the Kaiser-Frazer partnership went to Wall Street for not one but two major stock issues and all but overnight raised almost $54 million, a staggering amount for a car company that existed mostly on paper. (Adjusted for inflation, that would be roughly three-quarters of a billion dollars in 2017.) By virtually every measure save one, that cash could all but guarantee success. The one exception was what it took to break into the auto industry. As Detroit knew, the cost of making and selling cars—costs for steel, rubber, and glass, for employing vast workforces, for marketing, dealership networks, executive salaries, and more—ran into many multiples of what the Kaiser-Frazer team had raised.

So despite the public adulation coming their way, Detroit took measure of these newcomers and found them wanting. In January 1946, just six months or so into a partnership already glowing with cash and goodwill, Frazer hosted a dinner for Kaiser at the venerable Detroit Club. It was Kaiser's coming-out party in Detroit, and executives from other auto companies filled the ornate wood-paneled dining room, led by Chrysler's K. T. Keller and lots of GM people and suppliers. Kaiser, in his enthusiasm, made the audience grimace as he kept mistakenly referring to Keller as "my friend J. T," but his listeners' bile rose even more as Kaiser enthused about his plans to break into the industry. One supplier executive couldn't hold back. "Cr-r-r-ap!" he said loud enough to be heard.

Perhaps an even more telling comment was heard as Kaiser boasted of the $54 million he and Frazer had raised on Wall Street to fund their new company. As author David Halberstam recounted in his book *The Reckoning*, a rival executive at the dinner riposted to Kaiser's boasts, "Give that man one white chip," white being the lowest value chip in a poker game. That's what the old hands in the industry thought of Kaiser and his cash: the newcomer had raised barely enough to ante up in a high-stakes game. Some of Kaiser's own team privately thought as much, notably Clay Bedford, his manufacturing guru. In December 1945, Kaiser sent son Edgar and Bedford to Michigan to inspect Ford's Willow Run wartime bomber plant as well as other sites to get some ideas. Bedford spent a day touring

Ford's massive Rouge plant, in its day the biggest and most advanced manufacturing site in the world. "Henry," a misty-eyed Bedford told Kaiser when he returned, "I've seen a billion dollars' worth of equipment!"

Kaiser remained sanguine. "My God, Clay, that may be obsolete any day! That's just a billion dollars' worth of liability!"

"We raised a few flags," Bedford said later. "But nobody then recognized the depth of the flags we raised. Though we were unable to prove it, we thought our new partners were short of funds to do the job."

The cultural differences between Kaiser's California team and the Detroit elite extended to age, too. At one point, Kaiser hired Ed Hunt, an old hand in Detroit who had produced battle tanks at Chrysler during the war years. At the age of fifty-two, Hunt had been the youngest man on the Chrysler operations committee; at Kaiser-Frazer he was the oldest.

So Kaiser and Frazer and their team fell to work. The government proved eager to give them the giant Willow Run bomber plant that Ford had built for wartime production. Designed by famed Detroit architect Albert Kahn, the technocrat who enabled Henry Ford's visions to rise in concrete and steel, the plant had cost $100 million and was enormous enough to house even the dreams of a Ford or a Kaiser. The main building was 3,200 feet long and a quarter mile wide. Some sixteen million creosote floor blocks went into the construction, ten million bricks, eleven miles of fence, 8.5 miles of concrete roads, and more than 105,000 fluorescent lamps. There was parking for 15,300 cars, an infirmary, and even a chapel. The bomber plant was so well designed and organized that it produced levels of output unrivaled in history. At full production, the four-engine B-24 Liberator bombers rolled off the line at Willow Run at the rate of one per hour. Shuttle crews—often women—would taxi to the nearby runway, take off, circle the field to make sure nothing fell off, and fly off to deliver the planes to a war zone.

But Ford Motor Company had no interest in making planes after the war. Ceding what became a billion-dollar aerospace industry to the West Coast, Ford preferred to return to what it knew best—cars and trucks. Willow Run sat empty after the war, and Kaiser and Frazer were able to pick it up from the government's war surplus board at a relatively nominal rent. It was another stroke of luck for the pair, one of many that gave them confidence. When a reporter asked Kaiser, "Where are you going to get gears?" Kaiser answered, "It's funny you asked that question. Only today I turned to Edgar and said, 'Edgar, go buy me a gear factory.'"

But Kaiser and Frazer soon learned how much—or how little—their $54 million in Wall Street money would get them. Labor costs were going up; Walter Reuther, the visionary leader of the United Auto Workers, extracted richer contracts for his members from the Detroit automakers. Production costs ran to astronomical heights—$15 million for an engine line, another $10 million to build bumpers. Building a dealer network took time and money. And of course, an automaker had to keep building and selling year after year. There was never a time when the money-raising and money-spending would end. And what Kaiser and Frazer could spend was dwarfed by what the Detroit Three were spending. After the war, Ford Motor was spending $201 million and Chevrolet alone was spending $108 million for additional productive capacity.

Even with his problems, Kaiser got a good start, producing his first car just a year after the partnership with Frazer formed. But as early as 1947, a year after they started producing cars, Kaiser and Frazer had to borrow $12 million from the Bank of America, and their attempt for a third stock issue went nowhere when the underwriter withdrew at the last minute. Kaiser had to scrap plans for a new line of cars in 1949. That year, they made 58,000 cars and lost $39 million; in 1950 they made 151,000 cars but lost another $13 million. The end came in 1953, when Kaiser finally merged what was left of the effort into Willys-Overland.

It might be said that Henry Kaiser—founder of Kaiser Shipyards, Kaiser Steel, Kaiser Aluminum, and Kaiser Permanente health insurance firm for his workers—made just one mistake in his long and successful career: he had tried to be an entrepreneur in Detroit at a time when that was no longer possible.

"If you want to die a slow and painful death, be a small independent in the auto industry," Joe Frazer said once. And when it was all over, a rueful Henry Kaiser reflected on his experience. "I knew it would be hard and I knew we might not make it," he said, in a remark quoted by author Halberstam. "But I never thought we'd put so much in and it would disappear without a ripple."

Preston Tucker, Henry Kaiser, Joe Frazer—these were talented men with innovative concepts and exceptional determination. But it wasn't enough. Detroit in those postwar years, and for decades after, saw no need for entrepreneurs. Rather, the need ran to the opposite pole. Massive organizations with top-down leadership structures that scorned risk-takers as troublesome had proved not only desirable but necessary, foundational to success in the world's biggest and most complex manufacturing industry. Detroit had no use for anything else; indeed, it could not conceive a need for anything else.

Early in the twenty-first century, Dan Kildee, later a member of the US House of Representatives and a native of Flint, Michigan, the birthplace of General Motors and long an automotive capital second only to Detroit itself, remembered what it was like to grow up in a car town during that heyday of the giant automakers. "We were exporting cars to the world and importing cash," Kildee would say. "And we knew, really knew to a moral certainty that ought to frighten any other city that feels this way, *that it was never going to end.*"

CHAPTER 6:
CAFÉ NEW ORLEANS

“ **I** assure you I wasn't drinking when I decided, 'My God, I've got to take New Orleans back to Florida with me.'”

And so began Randal Charlton's three-year journey with Café New Orleans, at once the least typical part of his career but in some ways the most instructive part of his business education for what he later accomplished in Detroit.

"I'll say this for myself, I prepared well," he said later. Convinced that there needed to be a bit of Louisiana life and culture everywhere, he made several trips back to New Orleans, soaking in the atmosphere along with the hurricane cocktails invented at O'Brien's bar. He toured all the famous jazz clubs on Bourbon Street, Preservation Hall and the others, wept tears at the hot pepper festival on the bayou, took a cooking class for Cajun cuisine, lined up distributors of authentic Louisiana products like Blackened Voodoo beer and chicory coffee. He persuaded the cooks at Café du Monde in the French Quarter to allow him back in the kitchen to see how beignets were made. He studied the art of making po'boys and desserts. He bought prints by New Orleans artists and left Mardi Gras beads on the tables of his little Café New Orleans.

But if he aced the culture part, he pretty much flunked the business side. For starters, he mistook a trendy location for a profitable one. He rented an upstairs room on St. Armand's Key, just off Sarasota, for his restaurant. The famous Ringling Brothers circus owners had established St. Armand's decades earlier, building a little shopping strip there at which their wives could shop without having to go all the way back to New York. It was certainly trendy, but Charlton was shocked at how short the tourist season was. There was a burst of business around Thanksgiving, and another short one around Christmas, and then the snowbirds came down from January through April. The rest of the year it was dead. He hadn't done his market research—a cardinal sin as he would preach later to other entrepreneurs in Detroit. He also mistook his small, intimate space for one that could seat enough people to generate real cash. Café

New Orleans had twenty tables, so it could seat perhaps sixty people at a time, and, as Charlton learned, it needed a lot more than that to pay the bills.

Then there was trouble with the local building authorities. Getting permits took much longer than he had expected. Charlton wanted to put tables out on the sidewalk, but the city leaders of this older, wealthier community—staid, conservative Floridians—said "no." So he found himself hemmed in by local regulations and his own mistakes in judgment from the day the restaurant opened.

Even so, it was tremendously exciting for a long time. The tourists, in season, certainly had money to spend. St. Armand's was popular with celebrities. During the three years Charlton kept it open, Audrey Hepburn came in several times as did tennis star Steffi Graf, among others. People lined up outside the front door, but the café's small size meant the restaurant was consistently turning away customers. Further, Charlton discovered all the usual problems restaurants face. If the cook failed to show up, he cooked; if the dishwasher didn't show, he washed dishes. The café had a rapid cycle dishwashing machine that cleaned plates and glasses in ninety seconds, and more than once Charlton just stood over it, loading and unloading for hours. He was by turns maître d', waiter, busboy—whatever was needed.

And he promoted the hell out of it. He would stand outside on the sidewalk with one of the authentic New Orleans umbrellas they use in funeral processions, black with a red fringe, and invite passersby up. Once, he noticed a young couple on the beach across the way taking wedding photos, so he went over to ask where they were holding their reception. They weren't having one, so he invited them up and the kitchen cooked them special wedding beignets filled with mango fruit. Charlton did Sunday morning jazz brunches. He had engaged a New Orleans singer who packed in the crowds, but Charlton noticed people were so in thrall to her voice that they put down their forks just to listen. He had to tell her to take frequent breaks so people would eat up and make room for the next customers.

After about a year, the shortcomings of the business model began to wear. Charlton was exhausting himself, working seven days a week from eight in the morning until well after midnight. It was a punishing operation, and he dropped a lot of weight—at least thirty pounds—becoming thinner than any time since his teenage years, working on a farm in England.

With a mounting and dire cash shortage, he sold his house and looked for a cheaper place to live. When he opened the café, he owned a $350,000 upscale house on the bay; he sold that and moved to something much more modest on nearby Siesta Key. And he borrowed to cover the shortfalls in operations—borrowed from some gentlemen that a friend advised him had ways of collecting the debt no matter what. If that sounds a bit dramatic, it was indeed so. "I won't say they were leg breakers, just that I was assured they would get paid one way or the other," Charlton recalled later.

So the café became an endless round of sleep-deprived labor and worries over money. At the end of three years, it became obvious that there was no recovery possible. "We weren't making any progress," he said later. "I was a victim of my own self-inflicted lack of planning and my failure to understand my market." Café New Orleans had proven to be a popular location but was drowning in debt. The final irony is that it was filled on the day Charlton finally shut it down. He had musicians play "When the Saints Go Marching In" one last time, paid off his staff, cleaned up, and in the early morning hours headed to the beach on Siesta Key with a six-pack of beer and a full cargo of self-pity.

About the fourth or fifth beer, when he wasn't really caring, he caught a chill, and added to his problems by developing pneumonia. He was weeks getting over it. In the meantime, he had paid all his debts except for the big one to the . . . gentlemen who had their own ways of collecting. So he met with them and told them he had this house on Siesta Key that was worth the value of the loan. He told them he would turn over the deed to them for a dollar, and that settled that.

This once jet-setting entrepreneur who had visited half the nations in the world, hobnobbed with sheiks in the desert, and run cutting-edge biotechnology firms, was now without a job. He was also broke, homeless, ill, divorced, and exhausted, and he had no idea what he was going to do next.

CHAPTER 7:
DETROIT'S DOWNFALL

A thousand miles to the north, the city of Detroit, Michigan, was speeding toward its own dead end.

It started long before the early nineties. In the years immediately after World War II, American manufacturing stood triumphant, and few centers of industry felt more pride in their achievements and more confident facing the future than Detroit. Having produced the warplanes, tanks, and material that beat the fascists, Detroit was ready to produce civilian cars and trucks again. It did so with gusto, and thanks to the skilled efforts of labor leaders like Walter Reuther of the United Auto Workers, the benefits of American industrial might were widely shared even among the factory workers. Indeed, blue-collar wages ran so much above the national average that Detroit could boast it was the best place in the world to work on an assembly line.

But twin forces were at work undermining the city's prosperity. It took years for everyone to see it, and certainly hundreds of industrial cities large and small faced the same brutal trends of suburbanization and deindustrialization. But nowhere did the story play out more grimly than in the Motor City.

First, suburbanization. Even by the mid-1950s, cities were spreading out into the farmland and orchards beyond their borders. The American love affair with the automobile explains a lot of it, but there were many forces at work. Automakers and road builders were eager to sell more cars, and realtors and home builders touted the new subdivisions sprouting up almost overnight. Racism in all its ugly forms saw the white middle class heading to the exits for the newer suburban communities to the north of Detroit. In those communities, village and township officials welcomed all the new taxpayers and promoted ever more growth. The federal government subsidized this suburban sprawl with a variety of tax incentives and highway dollars, and, in a shameful episode, denied federally insured mortgages to African American neighborhoods in the central city. This discriminatory practice, or "redlining," helped to make the suburbanization process in

Detroit ugly and bitter. In time, suburbanization would drain away Detroit's population from a peak of 1.85 million in the 1950 census to about half that by the time Randal Charlton lost his restaurant in Florida. Eventually, the city's population would fall below 700,000, and flight to the suburbs would leave vast tracts of Detroit's 139-square-miles bleak and abandoned.

What suburban sprawl didn't kill, deindustrialization finished off.

Detroit's success in the first half of the twentieth century paved the way for its decline in the second half. All those factories that proved so innovative in the first decades of the century—Henry Ford's Highland Park plant or the Packard plant—were obsolete by the fifties; automakers built their replacement plants far from the city. Foreign competitors in autos, steel, and other products recovered from the devastation of World War II and began to outcompete US producers. Automation saw machines doing the labor of more and more factory hands. The once-lucrative paychecks were replaced by layoff notices.

Denial was the order of the day. American industrial might loomed so large on the international stage that Detroit automakers ignored, or belittled, the foreign competitors that began to sell their vehicles in the US market in the 1960s. But those little cars, even in their earliest boxiest styles (the Honda Civic, Toyota Tercel, the Datsun) proved attractive to a certain type of American buyer—one conscious of fuel costs and disdainful of ostentatious Detroit "land yachts" with fancy grills and tail fins; buyers who simply wanted a car that started every time, was small enough to park easily, and whose lack of traditional Detroit prestige didn't matter. Volkswagen, the most familiar of these imports in the early sixties, capitalized on this anti-Detroit feeling with its "Small is Beautiful" marketing campaign for its famed Beetle. The Japanese imports—Toyota, Nissan, Honda—more or less crept in under the radar.

Journalist David Halberstam, in his landmark book *The Reckoning*, which recounted the battle between the importers and the Detroit Three automakers, captured the way Detroit auto barons grossly underestimated their new competitors. As Halberstam tells it, in 1971, race driver Carroll Shelby was offered a big Toyota dealership in Houston, Texas. He asked his friend, the famed Lee Iacocca, father of the Ford Mustang and future savior of Chrysler, whether he should make the investment. "Let me give you the best advice you'll ever get. Don't take it," Iacocca said.

"Why not?" Shelby asked.

"Because we're going to kick their asses back into the Pacific Ocean," Iacocca said.

Shelby later estimated that taking Iacocca's advice cost him something like $10 million. Much worse: hundreds of thousands of Detroit workers and their families would pay dearly for such egotistical misjudgments.

The imports, as they were known, slowly but steadily stole away market share from the Big Three of General Motors, Ford, and Chrysler. In 1960, the Big Three, plus the smaller American Motors, owned 90 percent of the US vehicle market. By 1970 that had slipped to 82 percent—enough to get Detroit's attention but mostly just to scoff at the newcomers. By 1980, foreign carmakers owned 18 percent of the US market; by 1990 that rose to 25 percent, and to 30 percent by 2000. The first decade of the new century proved disastrous for the Detroit Three, with decades of mounting issues culminating in GM and Chrysler filing for bankruptcy in 2008 and Ford avoiding that only by mortgaging every asset it owned, down to its blue oval logo. By 2010, foreign automakers—Toyota, Honda, and Nissan, joined now by a smattering of smaller brands including Kia, Hyundai, and Subaru—owned more than half of the entire US vehicle market. And having entered the market forty years earlier by selling only the smallest fuel-efficient cars like the original Civic, the "transplants" (foreign-based carmakers operating their own factories in the States) could challenge the Detroit Three for the most lucrative segments of the market—the big SUVs and pickup trucks worth thousands of dollars in profit each.

And it didn't help that municipal leaders in Detroit's City Hall made about every mistake they could trying to stem the outflow of residents and jobs.

In 2013, this author, as a business reporter with the *Detroit Free Press*, cowrote with my *Free Press* colleague Nathan Bomey an in-depth study of the practices and mistakes that had put Detroit's municipal government into bankruptcy. Our report, headlined "How Detroit Went Broke," looked at fifty years of mismanagement of city government. Among the findings we published in the *Free Press* in September 2013:

Taxing Higher and Higher: City leaders tried repeatedly to reverse sliding revenue through new taxes. Despite a new income tax in 1962, a new utility tax in 1971, and a new casino revenue tax in 1999—not to mention several rate increases along the way—revenue in 2012 dollars fell 40 percent from 1962 to 2012. Higher taxes helped drive residents to the suburbs and drove away business. By the time Detroit filed for bankruptcy in mid-2013, the city wasn't taking in as much revenue from its multiple taxes as it did from property taxes alone in 1963.

Downsizing—Too Little, Too Late: The total assessed value of Detroit property—a good gauge of the city's tax base and its ability to pay bills—fell a staggering 77 percent over the past fifty years in 2012 dollars. But through 2004, the city cut only 28 percent of its workers, even though the money to pay them was drying up. Not until the last decade before bankruptcy did Detroit, in desperation, cut half its workforce. The city also failed to take advantage of efficiencies, such as new technology, that enabled enormous productivity gains in the broader economy.

Skyrocketing Employee Benefits: City leaders allowed legacy costs—the tab for retiree pensions and health care—to spiral out of control, even as the State of Michigan and private industry were pushing workers into less costly plans. That placed major stress on the budget and diverted money from services such as streetlights and public safety. Detroit's spending on retiree health care soared 46 percent from 2000 to 2012, even as its general fund revenue fell 20 percent.

Gifting a Billion in Bonuses: City pension officials handed out about $1 billion in bonuses from the city's two pension funds to retirees and active city workers from 1985 to 2008. That money—mostly in the form of the so-called "thirteenth check" in addition to the normal twelve monthly payments—could have shored up the funds and possibly prevented the city from filing for bankruptcy. If that money had been saved, it would have been worth, by one expert's estimate, more than $1.9 billion by the time of the bankruptcy filing to the city and pension funds.

Borrowing More and More: Detroit went on a binge starting around 2000 to close budget holes and to build infrastructure, more than doubling debt to $8 billion by 2012.

Adding the Last Straw—Kilpatrick's Gamble: Disgraced Mayor Kwame Kilpatrick is best known for a sex and perjury scandal that sent him to jail and a massive corruption scandal that sent him to federal prison. The corruption cases further eroded Detroit's image and distracted the city from its fiscal storm. But perhaps the greatest damage Kilpatrick did to the city's long-term stability was when he borrowed $1.44 billion in a flashy high-finance deal to restructure the city's pension fund debt. That deal, which could cost a staggering $2.8 billion over the next 22 years, represented nearly one-fifth of the city's debt at the bankruptcy filing.

———————————

Racism, factory closings, flight to the suburbs, municipal mismanagement—a toxic brew, indeed. The combined blows left Detroit drained, prostrated before history—the international symbol of Rust Belt ruin. Perhaps the only thing one might say in mitigation is that the losses opened the door for something new to replace the old model, if only Detroit could find a way.

CHAPTER 8:

CHARLTON'S WILDERNESS YEARS

After the closing of Café New Orleans, a friend stepped up to help. He put Charlton together with a colorful adventurer named David Rabhan, a Georgia businessman who once served as Jimmy Carter's pilot during Carter's 1970 run for governor. By turns an artist and a Special Forces major, Rabhan had business ventures all over the globe, but in the seventies, he had gotten caught up in the Iranian Revolution and was accused of being an American spy. The Iranians threw him in one of their prisons, where he spent ten years imprisoned, with long periods in solitary confinement. Carter, after he left the White House, wrote letters, trying to get his friend freed. Eventually, the Iranians relented (about the time Charlton was starting Café New Orleans), and Rabhan came home to Georgia to try to put his life back together. Rabhan had family money, and a huge ranch in Georgia with 10,000 head of cattle, a pecan orchard, and a commercial goat herd. He was looking for an assistant to help him run the place, and once the mutual friend introduced him to Charlton, Rabhan offered the job to him. Charlton, having recovered from pneumonia (if not from the emotional and financial turmoil of his losses), moved into the extensive home on the ranch.

Those days on the ranch, working outdoors with the herds, were a balm to Charlton's spirit. It recalled his childhood years on the farm in Devon. He spent a lot of time walking with Rabhan in the Georgia evenings. Rabhan spoke about his time in Iranian prisons—how, arrested in 1980, he had waited three years for his first court appearance, only to be charged with espionage. There followed years in chains, often blindfolded and shuttled from one prison to the next. He was beaten many times, tortured, subjected to mock executions. He kept his sanity by sketching scenes from memory or by making daily tea for his fellow inmates.

Years of confinement led him to choose a rather unusual house when he finally got home. One entire side of the house was glass, with an expansive view out to a lovely lake; it was as if he wanted no more constraints on what he could see. But Charlton found it tricky because even the bathroom wall was glass, and one day, as he was taking a late shower, he saw the postal carrier walking by with him in full view. Charlton hastily donned a towel.

When Rabhan finally came home from Iran, he was bitter, understandably, and driven to make up lost time in his business career. At that time, the US Department of Agriculture offered generous loans and grants for businesses large and small in rural America. Rabhan had various plans, including a scheme to set up an infant formula plant in South Africa, and one of Charlton's jobs, aside from managing his cattle herd and the ranch in general, was to draw up business plans for that and other ventures. He was happy to do that; working on the business plans got his business brain going again.

But Charlton had to admit that over time, he became concerned about some of Rabhan's business practices. So were many others. The US government indicted Rabhan, and he later pled guilty to conspiracy to commit bank fraud involving a $5 million guaranteed loan to build a catfish-processing plant in Georgia. He spent another four and a half years in prison, this time in the United States. But by that time, Charlton had long moved on. He left David's ranch after a year or so, one of the only times in his life he quit a job.

Charlton returned to Florida and lived in a small apartment in Oviedo, near Sarasota. He was in his midfifties by this time, almost five years past running a publicly held life sciences company, with a case of shaky finances and an even shakier confidence level. He thought he might return to his original calling as a writer. He nurtured an idea to write up the adventures of his father, Warwick Charlton—a one-time war correspondent with the British army in World War II who later, fascinated with the story of the Pilgrims at Plymouth Rock, built a full-size replica of the *Mayflower*, assembled a crew, and sailed it to America. So Charlton did that, and wrote perhaps a dozen short stories, joined a writer's support group, and got a few unpaid articles published in the *Orlando Sentinel*. But he couldn't find his way back to a writing career. He was trying to figure out what his next gig was going to be, and he wasn't making any progress.

There were a couple of short-term efforts. He worked as a salesman for a new company called Laser Sight, an early venture in laser eye surgery. He flew to Malta in the Mediterranean, where the intense sunlight and general lack of medical care had resulted in a lot of eye damage. He also visited the United Arab Emirates and Dubai. But the equipment, while

FDA approved, was still premature to find much acceptance. It was a hard sell. He took just one order in a year. While it was a substantial one, it was less than promising.

These were Charlton's wilderness years, almost a decade when little or nothing seemed to go right for him. Some of his failures were, in hindsight, amusing. He had the notion to sell low-fat beef to American burger chains. The whole country seemed to be joining the health craze; people were trying to eat right, or at least they desired to see more healthy items on even fast-food restaurant menus. He knew from his work with cattle that a variety called the Belgian Blue had been bred for the lowest fat content of any breed. So he worked up a business plan and lined up the supply of beef and started to make the rounds of burger chains. And he remembered the day that reality dawned: he was meeting with one major US fast-food chain, going on about the low-fat content of the Belgian Blue. The top executive in the meeting said to him, "Mr. Charlton, you don't seem to understand that fat is what holds our burgers together when cooked. Your beef could never be used for patties." Charlton was flummoxed, but he had to admit that he had not done enough market research before he went calling on potential customers.

Thereafter, he joined his father, Warwick, who was then in his late seventies and trying to set up a business deal in Moscow. Charlton went simply to help him out, but the idea flopped, and he didn't know what he was going to do next. He went back to Orlando. His confidence was eroding with each one of the 150 or so resumes that he mailed off, for which he got no reply. His batteries were flat, as he put it much later, his confidence at zero.

And the day came that he went to the local job center and put his hand on the door and couldn't go in. He didn't know what he was going to say. How could he explain that after running a series of life sciences companies, including a couple of successful public companies in the agricultural sciences, that now he wanted to see if they had any jobs as a night watchman so he could earn enough to pay for groceries? They'd even have to show him how to use the "torch," as the British call a flashlight. So he turned around and left, and he thought he'd sunk as low as he could go.

He lost touch with his friends. "I always wished I had closer contact with Charlton through the wilderness years," Alan Walton said later. "I more or less lost contact with him for a long time. He really didn't come back to my life for at least ten years. Even Christmas cards that I would send would come back 'addressee unknown.'"

Talking about this time in his life, Charlton's voice lowers, almost falters, as he begins to speak of his daughter, Catherine. Kate was beautiful, very smart, incredibly well-read, and a gifted poet even as a child. One of her poems was selected for inclusion in a book of poetry by English schoolchildren; she was nine or so when she wrote it.

But it was evident early on that Kate faced some challenges. She was dyslexic, so though she read everything, she had an odd way of writing—turning letters like P or K backward, or having words float on the page. She wrote some pretty macabre poetry as a child on themes of death. She grew into a young woman and attracted some less than desirable characters as friends; she got into drugs and was hospitalized a couple of times as a teen because of overdoses. She went to Manchester University and failed her first-year tests, which astonished everyone because she was so manifestly bright, but her dyslexia and other problems had done her in. Finally, when she was still college-age, she was diagnosed as suffering from schizophrenia, a terrible disease that is also very hard to understand or recognize when it first appears.

Despite all this, she qualified as a teacher and got a job teaching English as a foreign language in Italy. Charlton visited her in Sardinia for a few days. She had put her drug use behind her, and she appeared to have organized her life. Things were going well, and she seemed healthy and relatively happy. Soon, though, she came to back to England and stayed with Charlton's oldest daughter, Rachel. He later suspected she got back into drug use somewhere along the way. One day, while she was alone in the house, she swallowed a bottle of prescription pain pills and died.

"I cannot begin to convey the shock it is to a parent to lose a child in that way," Charlton said many years later. He went back to England and spent several months helping his eldest daughter, Rachel, move out of the house in which Kate had committed suicide. "It was a difficult time," he would later say.

Serendipity plays a role in all our lives, and perhaps in the lives of entrepreneurs most of all, because they must be tuned to opportunities as they arise. Back in Florida, he went to see a women's soccer game at Sun Stadium in Orlando. This was during the 1996 Olympic Games in Atlanta, but some of the events were held elsewhere. This event happened to be a consolation game between Denmark and Sweden—the two teams no longer in the running for medals, playing a game for the honor of it.

Charlton had always enjoyed football, as they call it in most of the rest of the world, but he understood that soccer was a minor sport at best in America. "I thought I might be sharing the stands with two men and a dog," he said later. "I was pleasantly shocked to see the huge crowd, and that instead of middle-aged soccer louts like we see in many European games, the crowd here were mostly young families, including their children." Charlton, who understood the game well, got talking to people next to him and started explaining what was going on; a lot of them didn't know the game and had just turned up to see an Olympic event. And at one point he said, "They're going to score now," and the team did score, and people turned to him and said, "How in the world did you know that?" Anyway, he started thinking about this market and doing some research, and he learned that something like seven million young women played soccer in America even then, which was more than the rest of the world put together.

At that point, he got interested in women's soccer as a potential market opportunity that everybody was overlooking. He set up, together with his sister, a company called the Red Squirrel Corporation; the name had no real meaning behind it any more than Apple has a meaning. The idea was to set up a website, looking ahead to the 1999 World Cup. He had a lot of fun producing a book, the first guide to women's soccer worldwide, to be distributed during the World Cup, and setting up a site that would sell advertising—www.womenssoccer247.com. He got his accreditation as a soccer journalist, turned up at the training grounds, followed the US women's team around the country, and got to know the players who would soon become famous, like Mia Hamm. He then wrote to every country in the world to find out if they were playing women's soccer, everywhere from American Samoa to Zambia. He learned a lot about what the American soccer movement was doing to encourage the quality of the game and better pay for women athletes. He built out the website and engaged a team of correspondents across the globe. No matter where you were in the world, you could find out what was happening in any country in women's soccer.

The website probably had more content than just about any other on women's soccer, but what it didn't have was revenue. This was early days, and advertisers were not yet convinced that the Internet was the place to go. Charlton and his sister had a small group of backers, but essentially they ran out of money. They did their best to get advertising but just couldn't get it. Maybe if he had tried it just a few years into the future, when Mia Hamm led the US team to the World Cup title in 1999 and then to Olympic Gold in 2004, they might have done better. But once again, as with some of his life sciences ventures, being first to market made him the most inventive, but not the most profitable.

In 1999 Charlton met his wife, Lee, in Detroit. They'd actually been correspondents. Lee was a lifelong pen pal writer, belonging to a society where the members wrote to people around the world to exchange ideas and talk about life. She had pen pals in Israel, Argentina, and elsewhere. She had, on one or two occasions when traveling, met some of them in person. And Charlton likewise had done some of that, too. So he and Lee started as pen pals, exchanging ideas. She was living in Detroit at the time. Born in Britain like Charlton, she'd been married and living in Texas when she divorced and moved north to Birmingham, a suburb of Detroit, to live with her daughter. Charlton, meanwhile, was living with his sister, Victoria, who put up her mostly penniless brother in her apartment in the Forest Hills section of Queens. She and Charlton corresponded a couple of years before they met during the time the World Cup was held in the United States, and Charlton was going to Chicago to see a game between the US and Brazil while he was working on his soccer book. He flew to Detroit and met Lee and then they drove the five-hour trip to Chicago together. Charlton was taking pictures for his website and the book, and they saw a couple of games together.

To say they hit it off is an understatement, and that their relationship would grow and thrive despite his troubles shows how durable their bond became. It started as a long-distance relationship; it became more geographically distant when his daughter, Kate, died and Charlton spent several months in England. He was pretty much broke when Kate died, and it became clear that he needed to stay in England to support the family. His other daughters were distraught, and Kate died in her sister Rachel's home in Oxford. Understandably, Rachel didn't want to stay there and told her father, "I can't live here, Dad, you've got to help me find another home." So that's what Charlton did, spending months helping her move. "That was in retrospect probably useful therapy for me to have something to do," he said much later. After he returned again to the US, he plowed himself back into the soccer book. The book could have been about plumbing or tulips; it didn't matter. The writing was therapy, although his confidence remained at low ebb.

"Unfortunately, when you lose a member of your family like Kate, it is almost impossible, I believe, not to take some guilt on board," Charlton said later. "It's heavy stuff and it stays with you. But I think what you have to do is learn from it." The one thing Charlton took from it, which helped him to regain his emotional footing at long last, was that he emerged from the sorrow of Kate's death determined to lose all social fear. Kate was very much a free spirit. She didn't worry about doing things that people might think were below her. Charlton could hear her telling him, "Dad, do something!"

And so he did.

Shortly thereafter, Charlton's friend, Alan Walton, who had recruited him for University Genetics many years earlier, came back into Charlton's life. They had lost touch during Charlton's wilderness years, but eventually, Walton tracked Charlton down and told him he might have a role for him in a new life sciences company he was thinking of starting, yet to be named. The idea was to help pharmaceutical companies do their early drug tests on actual human tissue as well as on lab animals. It would mean working with hospitals and medical schools to ethically source tissue samples from biopsies and other procedures and then supply these tissue samples to the drug firms that needed them for their research. Walton was still heading up his investment firm, Oxford Venture Partners, and this notion was just one of the ideas he was exploring. He was talking about putting up a half-million dollars for it, if and when it ever happened.

Not sure that anything would emerge from that idea, Charlton began to think about where he might find the lowest-cost space available for a start-up life sciences firm. And there seemed little doubt that the best bargains in America at the dawn of the twenty-first century were to be found in Detroit, Michigan. The city was filled with industrial facilities that were sitting empty; the local economy was so battered that people would do all they could to welcome a newcomer who might be able to create something. After an exploratory trip there, Charlton told Lee that Detroit was where they were going to try to create a new life.

But with the soccer effort busted, Charlton had to once again look for other means to keep body and soul together. That included working for a while in a flower shop, driving a delivery truck, and delivering phone books for minimum wage. ("Hey, it got me fit and I didn't have to think much about things when I was delivering them," he said later with his good humor back in form.) Alan Walton was yet to come through with anything definitive on the new venture, and many was the day Charlton asked himself, now approaching sixty years of age, "What the hell can I do with my life?"

This was hardly the career path one might expect from someone who had been a CEO with successful public corporations. But Charlton's confidence still was not high. However, having emerged from the tragedy of his daughter's death, he was so desperate to keep moving ahead that he was willing to do anything except sit at home and wait for the phone to ring. He decided that any action was better than no action, and that the best way to regain his confidence was to do something, anything. One day, he visited the Detroit Zoo, and noticing that some of the animals were in need of better care, he got the idea of becoming a zookeeper. So he went down to Detroit's City Hall and took the city's qualifying exam for a zookeeper's job. And since he had plenty of restaurant experience with Café New Orleans, he applied for another job as a sandwich-maker with a local restaurant.

And then came one of those days that keep entrepreneurs in the game. It was early spring of 2000 and Charlton received three jobs offers on the same day. One was to work as an animal keeper at the Detroit Zoo. The second was to make sandwiches at a suburban restaurant. The third call came from Alan Walton. He offered Charlton a job as CEO of his new life sciences company, with a $100,000 salary and an initial investment of $500,000 to get the firm up and running.

CHAPTER 9:

A NEW MODEL EMERGES FOR DETROIT

S
o at last the path of Randal Charlton, the expatriate Englishman fallen on hard times, began to merge with that of Detroit. The company that Charlton built in Detroit, and how he built it, were so unlike the familiar legends of Ford and Dodge and Chrysler that formed the Motor City's mythology that it's worth exploring in detail. Keep in mind that this tale was unfolding even as the broader city all around Charlton was sinking into the lowest depths of its despair. It offers not just one of the few bright economic stories in the city in the early 2000s, but a vision of a new entrepreneurial future that Detroit could embrace.

It started with that phone call from Alan Walton, whom you'll remember had recruited Charlton years before to run his University Genetics company when Charlton first came to the United States in the early eighties. Walton was British-born but a naturalized American; he was a professor of biotechnology at Case Western Reserve in Cleveland. And he was still running his venture capital firm, Oxford Venture Partners, investing in a variety of biotechnology firms. After their earlier connection, Walton had lost track of Charlton for years, but finally, in 1999 he tracked Charlton down and got him on the phone to pitch an idea for another company, something new in the biotechnology world.

Walton's idea was to help pharmaceutical companies develop new medicines faster and cheaper. Typically, as he explained to Charlton on the phone, pharmaceutical companies developed their new medicines in the lab and tested them first on animals; only the most promising moved on to human trials. The process was laborious and expensive; drug development could take years and cost hundreds of millions of dollars. Walton was suggesting that pharmaceutical firms might save time and money if they could skip some of the animal testing, which often proved unreliable; yet the government would never allow untested compounds to go straight to human trials. So, he suggested, what if promising new drugs could be tested not on live humans but on human *tissue*? There is an almost unlimited supply of human tissue available; it comes from routine biopsies that surgeons perform every day. Say a patient is having a biopsy for breast cancer or some other disease: the surgeon removes a bit of the suspected tumor, examines it, and discards the remaining tissue that's no longer needed. Walton's idea was to ethically source that discarded tissue, analyze it, freeze it, and offer it to pharmaceutical companies to use in drug tests.

As they each recalled the conversation later, Walton said in effect, "What we need to do is develop a bio bank." Walton's Oxford Venture Partners investment fund already had one company called Psychiatric Genomics, which he knew was near to Charlton's heart and to his as well; Walton's first wife, an Indian woman, had committed suicide when he was a professor at Case Western, and he knew Charlton had lost a daughter to schizophrenia. And he was setting up that company to look at the genetic causes of schizophrenia, manic depression, and other mental disorders. But he wanted to look at a broader spectrum of diseases, especially various types of cancers. Walton explained the severe limits on animal testing of new medicines: drug companies were using mice, rats, and pigs for their early stage tests, and a big problem for the drug companies was establishing that these animal tests were reliably going to show that the drug would work on humans. Creating the disease model in a lab mouse population is costly and time-consuming and often prone to poor results. If the target disease was known only in humans, then the animal models could not reliably be used to predict results. Various drugs that seemed promising up to the point of clinical trials turned out to be a bust when tried on humans. Walton believed that if he could ethically source human tissue samples, with the patients' permission, then that tissue could be used in the testing of new experimental drugs.

If anyone knew the challenges, it was Walton. He had been a major figure in the Human Genome Project, the $3-billion-dollar scientific effort to map the human genome. He knew the pitfalls of drug development, yet he also knew that business opportunities were beginning to emerge as a result of the genome project. He believed there was an opportunity to provide drug companies with a bio bank of high-quality human tissue samples from around the world for early stage testing of potential drugs.

Such a tissue bank could solve some of the vexing problems facing drugmakers, like the sometimes abrupt rise and fall of demand for certain types of tissue. Demand had soared for tissue samples needed for researching cystic fibrosis and Duchenne muscular dystrophy after a scientific breakthrough indicated rapid progress was possible. But demand might crash if progress seemed disappointing and researchers turned to other areas of study.

So they talked. And initially Charlton said, "Alan, why are you talking to me about this? I've been involved in animal genetics. What I know about human pathology could be written on the back of a postage stamp and there'd still be room for the Lord's Prayer." "Well," Walton said, "I'd like you to spend a few months exploring the issue with me." Much later, Walton would say of this initial conversation, "I guess I had to explain the science to him initially, but he latched on very quickly."

At that time, Charlton learned, there were three companies already involved in building bio banks, and all were well funded, collectively, to the tune of over $100 million. But Walton said all of them were focusing on collecting samples in the United States, and there was a need to collect worldwide because that was the way to get the best samples. For example, in the white South African population, there was a prevalence of schizophrenia and depression and various mental disorders. In Russia, the detection of breast cancer and other cancers was less advanced than in the United States, where most cancers are detected early. Only in other nations could he reliably get late-stage tumor samples. Walton told Charlton, "We need to build a *world* bank."

Again Charlton asked, "How does that make me a candidate?" And Walton told him, "You've been around the world and you know how to deal with many different cultures." Of course, Charlton had been to Russia and many other countries, and Walton knew that Charlton understood how to conduct himself in Arab countries. So Charlton said, "Okay, let's take a look at it," and he spent the next four or five months, as an unpaid consultant, looking into it, all while his soccer venture was falling apart and he was dealing with the tragedy of Kate's death and applying for minimum wage jobs.

If the project went ahead, there were at least four critical problems that would be Charlton's job to solve: he had to procure a range of human tissue samples from around the world; he had to create and enforce standard protocols for collection, storage, packing, shipping, and otherwise handling the samples; he had to organize the bio bank itself for the safe and long-term storage of samples; and he had to satisfy all the many and varied regulations dealing with the ethics and safety of clinical testing.

Charlton read, he talked to people, and he thought about the various aspects of the problem. He went back to Walton with his conclusion that, yes, it was possible. With a lot of hard work, it was possible to make a business go of it. And Walton, too, became sold on the idea, and he told Charlton that his Oxford Venture Partners would hire Charlton as CEO and bankroll this embryo start-up to the tune of $500,000.

Charlton knew that a half-million dollars would go nowhere for a life sciences company. He would need dramatically more than that; his competition had dramatically more. But more money would come in time if he could make a good start. So Charlton resolved to find the lowest-cost lab space in America to give his new firm the best chance of survival, of stretching Oxford's initial $500,000 as far as possible. Still living in Florida, he began to turn his eyes northward, toward an industrial heartland hollowed out by factory closings and job losses, where real estate was cheap and where elected officials were eager to help anyone who had an idea to create new jobs and new hope.

Charlton also talked with Walton about where to set up the company. "I suppose you want me to move to Boston," where Oxford Ventures Partners was located, he told Walton. Walton said, "No, rents are ridiculous here. You can't get labs for love or money. You have to pay students signing-on bonuses." Then he asked if Charlton had heard that the State of Michigan had committed to using money from the multi-billion-dollar tobacco settlement case to subsidize a life sciences industry. Michigan had a surplus of inexpensive industrial space that might suit the new venture due to the implosion of its traditional automotive industry. The state also boasted a motivated workforce accustomed to equipment testing, quality control procedures, and working to fine tolerances. Charlton's start-up idea may have looked like peanuts to a place like Boston, but the State of Michigan, eager to land new cutting-edge firms, quickly agreed to subsidize Charlton's travel and promotion at biotechnology conferences. The state's Michigan Economic Development Corporation team led him on a tour of the state's different cities. He went to Kalamazoo, Ann Arbor, to Grand Rapids— where the Van Andel Institute research site was just getting started—and to Detroit. In Detroit, a man named Fred Rineheardt of Wayne State University showed him around the lab space on the campus and the older industrial buildings nearby; it proved a pretty discouraging tour, with one older building leaking rain through the roof. Charlton found it depressing to see all the vacant buildings; none of the potential spaces Rineheardt showed him were anywhere near adequate. Trying to explain what he needed, Charlton asked Fred if he remembered the movie *10*, the one with Bo Derek and Dudley Moore, in which "ten" was used as a superlative. "I need the technical equivalent of a 10 to set up this lab," Charlton told him.

After looking some more, he had pretty much decided on the college town of Ann Arbor and a partnership with the University of Michigan (UM).

But it was based on a misreading of what he could get from a partnership with UM. What mattered to Charlton was how much technical and commercial support he would get. And initially, the pathologists at UM were really interested in collaborating. In hindsight this was a mistake for an entrepreneur, because while UM's pathology folks were among the best in the world, they were also the busiest and had little time to spend on this upstart entrepreneurial venture; it would obviously be lowest on their list of priorities. Charlton signed a deal with them (fortunately, it had an exit clause) and he and Lee rented an apartment for a year in Ann Arbor. This was in May 2000, and he and Lee were moving in, using a rental truck and moving themselves to save money. The phone was still sitting on the floor when it rang and Fred Rineheardt of Wayne State University said, "I know everything I've shown you up to date hasn't interested you, but is it too late? I have a perfect ten." He explained it all to Charlton, who put the phone down and said to Lee, "Honey, I'm sorry, I know we just moved in, but I think we're going to have to move out." Understanding spouses are a blessing for an entrepreneur.

Charlton went to see Rineheardt and he indeed had a perfect ten. He showed Charlton the labs at the just-opened Karmanos Cancer Institute on Wayne State's campus in Detroit's Midtown district, and they were indeed state of the art. There was a whole floor empty, waiting for tenants. Charlton's start-up firm could use the space until WSU and Karmanos researchers needed it, but Rineheardt made clear that would be at least a couple of years away. He said, "You can have one lab and then you can expand into a second whenever you need it, and a third when you need it. And we'll give you an agreement with Wayne State University to give you technical support. And we will help you with hiring with access to our HR files to point you in the direction of anybody who might be lab techs." Charlton didn't even have any of Oxford's money in hand, but he knew he needed a deal like this. Oxford's funding wouldn't total all that much, certainly not compared to what his flush-with-cash competitors had to work with. So Charlton signed a deal and the still nameless start-up firm, comprised of Charlton and his one lab assistant, Kim, moved in on September 1, 2000.

That lab assistant, Kim Reed, had grown up in East St. Louis, Illinois, another hard-luck industrial town, a smaller version of Detroit. Different from many in her town, she graduated from Southern Illinois University with a degree in biological sciences, worked for a pharmaceutical firm in Iowa City, Iowa, for three years, then moved to Detroit, about the same time Charlton did, when her husband got an engineering job in the city.

Reed, then in her midtwenties, saw a want ad in the Detroit newspapers for a receptionist at the new Karmanos Cancer Institute. She had no interest in a receptionist position, but she figured the intake office at Karmanos would pass along her resume to the right person in research. Instead it went straight to the reject pile. There, Dr. Jim Eliason, another entrepreneurial researcher with a lab at Karmanos who had befriended Charlton early on, plucked her resume out of the pile and offered it to Charlton, who promptly hired her. (She thus became the latest example in our story of a person or place discarded by others and then given a second chance and making the most of it.)

"When I got there like literally it was an empty room," she recalled of those early days on the top floor of the Karmanos labs. "There wasn't even a phone in there. I don't know if I even had a chair!" Her first job, she learned, was to equip the lab from the ground up. Eliason gave her a catalogue from which to order lab equipment, so she started with that. But so open-ended was her task, and the prospects for this new start-up were so uncertain, that she wavered that first day. Talking to her husband about it, she remembers the tears coming as she confessed, "I think I made a mistake. There's nothing here. There's no one around. The place doesn't even have a phone." Her husband soothed her fears. "I remember him being calming, saying, 'If anyone can get that place into shape, it's you. You make things out of nothing many times.' And that was the motivation I needed."

It helped that Charlton turned out to be like no other boss she'd ever had. Charlton was putting to good use every business lesson he'd ever learned in a forty-year career, and his emotional quotient came to the fore, too. Whether it was the losses and pain of the previous decade or his natural affability, Charlton displayed an empathy and comradeship rare for start-ups.

"He's one of the most humble human beings I've ever met," Reed said later. "If he needed to help be the janitor, he would help be the janitor. I just remember when we would get equipment in, it was nothing for him to help me unpack boxes. 'What do you need me to do?' Every day he would always ask me what did I need him to do."

There at the very beginning, when Reed was sitting almost alone in that big lab, Charlton asked if he could sit near her to make a phone call.

"And I was like, 'Sure.' It shocked me. He was asking me if he could sit there and he was CEO of the company. Why is he asking me? I think he asked me that maybe two more times during the day. Finally, he asked me like a third time and I was like, 'Mr. Charlton, you know you're the CEO, right? You don't have to ask me to sit down. It's *your* chair.' And he was like, 'This is *your* lab.'

"That was the first time I really had worked for an employer that made me feel I wasn't just working for him, like what I did counted," Reed said later. "He demonstrated that. That never changed throughout his entire time as CEO. He always treated all of our employees as if they mattered. He would remember your kids and your spouses, and if he couldn't remember names, at least he would remember if you had a son or a daughter."

At this time, so close on the heels to his lost decade, Charlton's confidence remained shaky. But two incidents at the very beginning helped rebuild that confidence. Very early on, he had attended a meeting with Oxford's board in Boston. These were the people who would decide whether and with how much money to fund the venture. He wanted to impress upon them that he would be a wise steward of their cash, to demonstrate his frugality. He tried to get a hotel, but the cheapest hotel room he could get for one night was something like $450 at the Copley Plaza. So he called one of the Oxford partners, Stella Sung, and asked her if she had a spare room in her home. She did but wondered why. And Charlton told her, "I'd like to use it tonight if I may. I'm coming up for this meeting tomorrow. You're going to get me up at 4:30 for the meeting, which was in Connecticut. I'm not getting in until ten o'clock tonight. I'm not spending $450 of Oxford's money on a hotel room for just a few hours." Well, she loved that, and she told all her partners. That little single act helped established Charlton's reputation.

This was Charlton's first board meeting with the investors, and they hadn't yet put up any money; it was still just a concept. He was pretty nervous, and he was still one step away from broke. Lee was working as a medical transcriptionist to support them. But Charlton remembered another of his personal rules—there's a good reason why airline pilots don't wear Grateful Dead T-shirts or earrings, or have their hair cut in a funny way. They dress in a military-like uniform because that inspires confidence. And Charlton believed that was true of business, too. So Lee fitted him out with a designer suit she'd bought second-hand in the Grosse Pointe Goodwill thrift shop for about $20 and a tie she bought for a dollar. When Stella Sung met Charlton at the Boston airport, Stella commented on his sharp suit. Then she grabbed his tie and turned it over and read out the name of the designer brand and she said, "You'll do!" He told her the truth, which was that his wife had bought it at a charity shop for a dollar. And she said, "Yes, and the rest!" She didn't believe it. He took a lesson from that. It's one thing to look like Steve Jobs in jeans and a turtleneck when you're young or already very successful, but as you get older or you're starting out, you've got to look as smart as you can be. "You've got to look professional," he said later. He carried that lesson through at the firm, always wearing a suit and tie. He didn't insist on a dress code, but as the firm gradually added one employee a month (as they did for six years), it helped create a culture of being the best they could be.

Another incident at the very beginning also gave him a boost. When he and Lee committed to Detroit and this new venture, Charlton promised that he would promote this company any way that he could. Anytime anybody invited him to speak, he told her, he would accept, even though he didn't yet know much about pathology and the unnamed company was just a gleam in his eye. He got a call from people affiliated with the famous Technion Institute in Israel who were setting up an event at a library in suburban Bloomfield Hills, a wealthy suburb north of Detroit; they invited him to speak on his new venture. He got to Bloomfield Hills, thinking it was going to be three ladies and a dog, and he found the library was filled with people of high net worth. The organizer told him there were two scientists from Israel, including one who had been nominated for a Nobel Prize, who would speak first. And he was the third.

He was terrified. He hadn't yet set up the company. He had an empty lab with virtually no staff. He hadn't begun traveling. And in some ways, he didn't know what he was talking about. He was staring down lots of unanswered questions: Could they get samples? Would companies recognize their value for drug research? He told Lee, who was there with him, "You've got to stare at me and will me not to faint because I have never been so nervous in my life."

But as the first two scientists spoke, he learned another lesson. They were great scientists, clearly, but they talked as though they were addressing a scientific audience about the early stages of stem cell research. Charlton could tell the audience was bewildered. When it was Charlton's turn, he explained what he was trying to do in words of one or two syllables: he was trying to build a bank of tissue samples to aid in drug discoveries. He explained that mice were not men, and firms had been using mice, rats, and dogs for years in drug research and often it didn't work and sometimes there were horrific problems with drugs tested only on animals. When he sat down, he got a burst of applause that shocked him. That stayed with him, and from that time on he was always willing to put himself out there with a feeling that he could do this. He might fall flat on his face, but he also might spread the word about his company, and it was an inexpensive way to do it. So he made himself available whenever anybody asked, and he did all the media interviews he could. Sometimes he would go home from an interview and wonder what coverage would appear, but he found that the media would give him a fair ride for the most part, and that helped the new company enormously over the years by creating a culture of being completely open.

Charlton's original name for the company was Bio-SampleX, which he thought was a smart name. But one night, during a business trip to South Africa to pursue deals for tissue samples from hospitals, Stella Sung of Oxford called him with worry in her voice. Somebody had set up a website called BioSample.com, without the "X," and they had researched Charlton's new company and found that Oxford had deep pockets, so they sued for infringement on the name. Oxford's attorneys noted that Charlton had developed Bio-SampleX at roughly the same time and they advised that they could probably win this case, but Stella said, "Look, we're not interested in going into federal court, change the name!" So when Charlton got back from South Africa, he spent two weeks researching potential names to avoid this problem recurring. He started with Greek and Latin names. He went through all the medical-sounding names. Every name he or his staffers thought of was in use. So one Friday, he advised his small staff to come up with a name that meant nothing. Since the three founders were Alan Walton, Stella Sung, and Randal Charlton, he took the first syllables from each name to form "Alsterand." He went around the office, asking what everyone thought of this name; his Chinese biologist said that Chinese people could not pronounce "l." So Charlton dropped the "l" and the company came to be called Asterand.

Charlton also needed a logo for the company, and he didn't want something clichéd like a double helix. He looked though pictures and images and found instead exotic butterflies that he went with.

From the very beginning, Charlton recognized the only thing he could control was costs. Earlier in his career, before his Café New Orleans went bust, he would take taxis instead of public transit on business trips and order expensive suits instead of buying clothes at the thrift shop. It's not that he was extravagant, but he didn't pinch pennies. But now he tried to use all the miserable experiences of the previous years to make as much progress as possible with that first $500,000. Each day he posted on a bulletin board the number of days the firm had left before the cash ran out. It instilled a sense of urgency in the staff. His staffers would say, "Charlton, we have only seventy-five days cash left, get out of here and get on the road."

There were other steps. His staffing contracts with his workers ran for only ninety days at a time so as not to burden the young company with long-term deals. He always traveled coach when flying. When he started going around the world looking for partnerships with hospitals, if he could sleep on the couch of a friend of a friend, he did. He looked for the cheapest fares and the most reasonable accommodations he could find. "I think there's a lesson there for people using other people's money," he said later. "It's very difficult to treat other people's money like your own. And the closer you can get to doing that, I think the more successful you're going to be."

Charlton wanted to build a team of people that collectively took ownership of Asterand. After every board meeting at Oxford, he would have a staff meeting and he would explain to the workers what the board had decided. "There are very few things in businesses that have to be kept secret," he would say. "The formula of Coke is one, of course, and certain things that are patented. But businessmen can be way over secretive. I would address the staff as shareholders, because they were; all of them had share options. Even summer interns would get a nominal amount; every single one had share options. We had share options in place as well as a performance bonus, an annual target of sales. It paid out, not every year but it did. I think that worked incredibly well in developing a sense of loyalty and a sense of ownership and a level of confidence."

He'd also learned over the years what a negative influence on company morale perks can be if the CEO indulges himself. So he always made sure that his office was not the biggest—it was just another lab desk in the common, open space. That was intentional; it was part of managing the company and a way of sending a subliminal signal to the other employees that he wasn't in any way taking advantage of his position. Much later, when the company left the Karmanos Institute and moved into TechTown, the new business incubator at Wayne State University, he let his HR manager organize the space, and she built in a big corner office for him. He never moved in. Rather he told her to put two people in there. "It's a management style that not everyone will buy into, but I think it's appropriate for today's world," he said.

And Charlton was the lowest paid CEO in Oxford Venture Partner's portfolio of fifty or so start-up companies; he made about $120,000 in his first year. Oxford then gave him a raise to $160,000. He didn't refuse it; he wasn't stupid. But he was thinking long-term, and he knew what his drawbacks were. He knew if he asked for $300,000 he'd probably get it, but he also knew that that would make it easier for them to replace him. He wanted to be with this company until it was successful.

He also had another rule—there had to be someone in the company who made more than him. Not just for symbolic reasons but for good business reasons. The sales force drove every company, and he knew he had to bring in salespeople that would be paid partly on commission. And he was totally prepared for the best salesperson in the company to earn more than he did with their salary and commissions. That would be living proof that they were successful.

"It's a bit like managing a professional football team," he would say. "The coach on the sidelines is calling the shots, but his quarterback is earning considerably more. The CEO is not the quarterback. He's the coach. He's not on the playing field. In a company like Asterand, the quarterback is either your chief scientist or your head of marketing or your vice president of sales. They're on the front line."

Kim Reed remembers that Charlton would frequently say, "'I'm not a scientist. I'm a businessman, but I have this funny knack of hiring people who are qualified to do the job. I don't have to do know how to do science. I just have to know how to hire the right people.' He would always say that."

That first Christmas, Charlton handed Kim a bonus check for $1,000, telling her how much he appreciated her hard work. "I had never gotten a bonus or gift like that," she said. "And the way he handed it to me, 'I wish I could give you more.' I couldn't believe I was that appreciated. He was that way. He was always very appreciative of all the employees."

The firm also nurtured a culture of giving other people credit where they deserved it. Charlton was always careful whenever he was talking about Asterand to let people know the firm was on the campus of Wayne State University and that it had support from the Michigan Economic Development Corporation. He put it in press releases, mentioning support from the City of Detroit, for example. "I think there's a lesson there," he said. "A lot of entrepreneurs think they did it all and they forget the organizations that helped them. And if they can only remember them when they talk in public, it comes back to them a hundredfold."

So Charlton made that first $500,000 last. There was one conference room on the fifth floor at Karmanos, and Charlton and his team shared it with other Wayne State scientists. When the conference room was booked, they'd have their meetings wherever they could. On more than a few occasions, it was in the stairwell, or down in the coffee shop. Stella Sung or Alan Walton at Oxford would call now and then and say, "You probably need more money now, don't you?" and Charlton would say, "No, not yet." They were bemused that their first $500,000 was lasting so long. It lasted nearly a year, even with six people on the staff and all the travel Charlton was doing.

The challenges of collecting tissue samples from around the world were daunting. Among them, Charlton had to ensure the samples were collected ethically with patient consent; there could never be a whiff of black market activity. Next, collecting tissue samples by the thousands from around the world would demand the cooperation of people in multiple hospitals, yet not interfere with their daily operations. Charlton also had to make sure the data identifying each tissue sample was correct and that he could get the samples into the biobank in a time-sensitive way that maintained their integrity.

So Charlton, the veteran road warrior, began to set up relationships with hospitals in Russia, China, South Africa, Malta, and, at home, with Wayne State University, to go through the process of getting ethical approval and then getting initial samples. And the way he did it was to say at each stop, whether Moscow or Malta, "Look, I don't want to sign a big contract, let's do a test, and if it works for you and us, we'll go into a longer-term agreement." And that worked because it made it easier for the hospitals he was dealing with to approve something quickly. Each was just going to send in one shipment from Russia, South Africa, Malta or wherever until the firm had established itself. To solve the problem of the workload at all the various collection sites, Asterand would pay the salaries for a nurse and a technician in each pathology lab of the participating hospitals. The nurse and technician would collect the tissue samples, ensure patient consent, fill out the forms, and get the samples packaged and shipped to Detroit. When they were not collecting Asterand's samples, the nurse and technician would work their regular duties. Charlton additionally offered to share the firm's database with the participating hospitals to support their own research.

To set the deals up, he flew economy class and slept on the couch of a friend in Moscow or wherever to save on a hotel. When he went to China, he stayed in Beijing for more than a week and paid less than it would have cost him to stay two nights in Boston at the Copley Plaza; his hotel was $50 a night, and by booking carefully, he got a round-trip air ticket for $500. It cost him about $900 for the whole trip to China. So by the end of that first year, he'd gotten a lot of samples ready to come in during early 2001 and he hadn't depleted the initial $500,000 investment.

And yet it nearly all came undone by Christmas of 2000, just a few months after launching the start-up, even though he had his first important shipment coming in from China with tissue samples. With Charlton's knowledge of importing and exporting, the one thing he insisted upon was that wherever the material came from, the first port of entry needed to be Detroit. This may sound trivial, but that's where it would clear customs. If something was shipped from London to New York and then on to Detroit, it would clear customs in New York, and there it might sit and sit and sit, particularly if it wasn't for a New York customer. The clearance agencies in New York would look after their own people. So if the shipment was coming from Moscow, with no direct flight to Detroit, he'd have it routed from Moscow to Amsterdam and then from there on a direct flight to Detroit. Getting this right was his priority, because he wasn't sure at the beginning if he could even get the samples to Detroit; logistics were still at that basic level.

The second priority was standardizing the process used to collect the samples, so that what people in Russia did would be what the people did in Malta and South Africa and America. Additionally, Charlton's team had to create a small cassette or casing for each tissue sample taken so that it could be shipped to Detroit; a typical box a foot or so square might hold 500 tissue samples. Alongside proving that he could get the samples shipped, the type of packaging and labeling and the amount of dry ice and the number of days in transit were all issues that he had to work out. They started by testing boxes filled only with dry ice, shipping them from Moscow to Detroit.

It came to that first Christmas and Charlton had one of his first big shipments of tissue samples due in from China. He had committed to pay for it, and the documentation said it had arrived in Detroit. He personally went down to the airport to collect items in those days. So he got to know the customs people and the airline people at Northwest Airlines, then the main carrier at Detroit Metro Airport. "And I went down to get my box from China and they couldn't find it," he recalled. The timing would prove awful to lose a shipment at this point. In a couple of weeks, he was planning to go back to Alan Walton to plan for the next tranche of funds, saying he had proved out the concept and the operational side. "And I was afraid to tell them that not only could I not get a shipment in, but that I had completely lost one," he said.

It was somewhere around December 15 when the shipment went missing. There was a ten-day period when the Northwest people did their best to find it. Charlton got increasingly frantic. He offered a prize of $1,000 to anybody at Northwest who could find it. The reward was published on Northwest's internal bulletin board. They weren't supposed to, but they let him in on the night shift when it was quieter, and he and Northwest people went up and down all the boxes in Northwest's huge facility at the Detroit airport looking for it.

On Christmas Eve, his friend Jim Eliason invited Lee and Randal over for Christmas dinner. Charlton had kind of given up on the shipment; it was going to be a gloomy Christmas. But the Northwest people all had his cell phone number, and he had told them to ring him day or night. And his phone rang and somebody from Northwest said, "How soon can you get here?" And Charlton said, "Twenty minutes or half an hour." And they said, "We've found your box." What had happened was that there had been a massive snowstorm around the fifteenth, when the box was unloaded, and it had fallen off the back of one of those trucks with the ramps they used to unload cargo. His box had fallen off into a pile of snow and gotten buried there. Finally, they had found it.

"I was filled with fear that being lost for so many days had ruined my samples," he said later. "We had our suppliers packing the tissue samples in dry ice, but of course that isn't meant to last more than a few days for delivery purposes. So as I drove to the airport Christmas Eve night, I called Jim Eliason and he said he'd meet me in our lab at the Karmanos Cancer Institute." Charlton thought there would be no way that the tissue samples could still be good because the package had gone way beyond the expected duration of the dry ice. But he hadn't counted on the box being buried in snow for ten days. So he and Jim rushed in, opened the box, and although there wasn't much dry ice left, mostly shards, they found that the tissue samples were still frozen. "So we popped it right into the freezer and then we repaired to Jim Eliason's home where we consumed large amounts of wine," he said.

That was an interesting first drama, but it was hardly the last. The hardest part at first was convincing foreign hospitals to do business with Charlton's firm. "Picture me walking into the largest cancer hospital in Moscow, which I did, and meeting with Professor Dr. Davidoff, the head of it, in his enormous Russian-style boardroom, and trying to convince him to do business with this little American start-up company," Charlton said. "He was very curt with me; he hardly looked up from his desk." Charlton knew, from many years' experience, the value of credibility at moments like this; it's like saying, "I'm here at the suggestion of the British Embassy." So when he started the company, he had insisted on it being embedded within a major university. And he had photographs of Wayne State University and the Karmanos Cancer Institute with him. So when someone like Professor Davidoff showed no interest, Charlton would say, "Let me show you where I'm based." That was important, not just in Russia but around the world, to say he was collaborating with people who already had a reputation. That's advice Charlton gives to start-up companies—to find a partner that already has a reputation and is ready to share it with you. "And you've got to give your partner organizations, like Wayne State University in my case, something in return, which I did, which was share options," he said.

That was one important thing. Another was to really understand how to do business overseas. A case in point was the agreement that he made with the Russians; it would not withstand scrutiny by any American attorney because it said almost nothing really, other than a general desire to collaborate on scientific research. "This is lesson number one and why Alan Walton thought I was the man for him," Charlton said. "I knew from working in Moscow before that if Professor Davidoff received any money from me under our agreement, an identical amount would be trimmed off his budget from the central committee. So there would be no benefit for his hospital to working with us." So the contract they signed had to look like a completely vanilla agreement with no benefit for his hospital so that his budget would not be affected negatively. And that's exactly how they did it. Charlton never showed the agreement to anybody in America until years later. But that speaks to the whole task of doing business internationally. "You've got to understand what the other side needs," he said.

As the tissue samples from around the world began to come in, Charlton got his first order for product from the major pharmaceutical firm Amgen in December of 2000. Amgen was one of the biggest biotech companies in America, based in Thousand Oaks, California. Charlton knew they would be an ideal leading customer for Asterand because, first, his firm could really help them if his team got everything right, and, second, the prestige of that connection would help him with other customers. Amgen is a leading developer of therapeutics in the biotechnology industry, and Charlton thought they would find his biobank of tissue samples a godsend for their preclinical testing and their investigation of new pharmaceutical therapies. These new drug treatments took an excruciatingly long time to develop. The average time to market in the industry was thirteen and a half years. Amgen's average drug development costs were $1.8 billion. If Charlton could help them reduce the time and expense needed in the process, he'd be handing them a major advantage. And their loyalty as a customer would show Asterand's investors that a human tissue bank could be a going concern and worth their investment capital. Indeed, landing a major account like Amgen was critical to the firm's success on every level.

Even so, when Charlton got the introduction to Amgen from Alan Walton, at first he didn't want the order because it was too big too early. He was still proving the concept. He was just starting to get the material in. He'd only started the company a few months earlier in September. But Walton and the other investors were anxious that Charlton not only test the firm's ability to get samples in from around the world, but that he test the concept by selling samples to a major customer. That initial order was only for ten samples. Yet Charlton knew his firm wasn't ready; they hadn't worked out all the details. Among them: once Asterand got the samples in, they would have to ensure that the samples were what they're supposed to be. If a Russian pathologist diagnosed a tissue as indicating stage 3 cancer, well, was it really that? Or was it stage 2? The standards might not be applied evenly across national borders. So there was a question of validating the data.

These fears were well-grounded. When Charlton shipped that first small order to Amgen, it almost cost him his company. Charlton shipped it out on a Friday, and the head of tissue acquisition called him up on Monday, and said, "Do you realize what you've done? Look, we're shut on Saturday and Sunday. All we've got here is security guards. Your samples came in on Saturday morning and they didn't know what to do with them. So it sat and that's totally unacceptable."

Charlton tried again, and again got it wrong. The second shipment to Amgen failed because the genetic analysis that accompanied the order was not precise enough; Charlton had to eventually establish industry-leading systems for analyzing and reporting RNA content. On the third attempt to get it right, the shipment was poorly packaged. And there were other things that were totally unacceptable. "We got just about everything wrong," he said later.

This scenario had, in, fact, been Charlton's nightmare from the very beginning. He knew that drug firms have whole divisions developing animal tissues as substitutes for human tissue and they wouldn't jump at Charlton's upstart idea. One potential customer scoffed at the idea, telling Charlton, "You just can't rely on your tissue-bank material. You don't know how it was frozen, when it was frozen, or even if it is the right sample! Customers are better off sticking with their regular way of testing on animal models, rather than going to Asterand."

So as Amgen complained each time about the successive screw-ups, Charlton would say, "Okay, we're very sorry. We'll do it again." Charlton delivered that order four times at no charge to Amgen. And then the head of pathology at Amgen's Thousand Oaks, California, facility, Dr. Ildiko Sirosi, called him and said, "I'm going to email you a copy of a memo that I'm going to send around to our departments worldwide which is going to detail the problems we've had with you, and it's going to advise everyone in Amgen never to deal with you again."

So Charlton said, "Well, I respect your right to do that and I understand why you've taken this view. But let me tell you what I would like to do. I'm going to keep delivering that order until you tell me that we've got it right." And that's what he did.

He had hired a full-time pathologist to visit each of the collection hospitals in the network to train the local pathologists on Asterand protocols and on-site diagnostic standards. It slowed down the tissue collection for a while, but the quality rose sharply.

"So I think we delivered that first Amgen order six or seven times before we got it right," Charlton said later. "And that taught me something really important that I learned late in my life—the importance of honest feedback. You have to keep interacting with your early stage customers to get it right."

And once Asterand finally got it right, Sirosi and Amgen became Asterand's number one customer over many years. And when Sirosi was up for promotion to director level and she had to provide an outside reference, she asked Charlton to provide it, which he did with pleasure. Tragically, she died of cancer a few years later, but her brutal criticism of everything Charlton and his team had delivered enabled them to refine what they were doing.

After that first Amgen experience, Charlton knew he couldn't keep making the same mistakes. He told his team they had to have some charter customers. So he went to drugmakers and said we think we're doing it right, but you're the customer and you will tell us if we're doing it right. During this period, if you can give us feedback, we will make you preferred customers. If there's a particular type of tissue that's difficult to get, we will give you the first rights to it when we obtain it.

"So there was this hilarious day over at Biogen Idec when we went over to talk to them, and they were interested in giving us an order of $200,000 worth of samples that they needed, and I said, 'No, we don't want an order that big right off the bat, we'd much prefer an order for $20,000 to prove that we can do it, and then we would be delighted to get the balance of the order.'" That was counterintuitive when a start-up is desperate to keep the company going. And that order would have meant so much to Charlton's young firm. But he also knew it could be a millstone around his neck if he got it wrong after the Amgen experience.

So Charlton got up this approach of going to potential customers, who were virtually all big international drug companies, and being completely up-front with them about how small his young firm was, what it could do and what it couldn't, and engaging them, saying, "Look, we want to understand what you need, we're not certain we can provide it, we think we can but we want feedback from you."

"Although it's scary," he would tell other entrepreneurs, "your customers will tell you the raw truth in a way that your wife and your family and your business partners won't. Test marketing and the value of it cannot be overestimated. There's a terrible tendency for early stage companies to keep trying to perfect what they're doing internally and not getting it out into the market, and while they're doing that, they're burning up cash.

"You have to have been through the mill. When I was thirty-one, and I first went into business and we started to get customers, we would go to big organizations and we'd get an order and we'd come away happy. What we didn't realize is that big organizations very often gave new companies really difficult-to-solve orders that their regular suppliers couldn't deal with. So they'd say, let's try this on these guys. If they can do it, we'll use them. That's an important lesson. You've got to be really wary of being given impossible tasks. You've got to stick to your knitting.

"If you go into a McDonald's now and ask for some weird concoction you can get at Starbucks, they'll say 'No, we've got this or that.' They're not going to do a double skinny mocha whatever because they're not set up to do it. When you're starting, people come at you and say can you do a double skinny mocha whatever, there's a terrible tendency to say, 'Could we, could we?' You lose your focus. So you've got to have that youthful enthusiasm and you've got to be immune to rejection and not take it personally, but you've also got to be aware of what your limitations are. In the early stages, I made it clear that we would stick to our knitting. So when people asked us to do impossible stuff, we'd say no we couldn't. That's a lesson for early-stage businesses. You can be easily seduced by the big order or the big deal before you're really ready for it. And we all have a learning curve, and small companies in particular have a learning curve."

And work it did. Charlton added, almost like clockwork, one new employee per month to his staff. By the end of 2000 he had five, and at the end of the following year he had seventeen, and he added another twelve in the year after that. He had more than seventy at the end of six years. And the orders grew and grew. In his shortened first year, with his Amgen order he did $10,000 in revenue, then the second year, in 2001, he did $100,000 for them, and the third year, $1 million. And so it went. By 2004, Charlton was supplying more than $4 million in tissue samples to Amgen alone.

At this point, the surprising and unexpected growth of Asterand offered one of the few signs of hope in Detroit's very bleak landscape. The city's mayor, Kwame Kilpatrick, was headed for his dramatic downfall, eventually going to prison for perjury and then corruption in office, along with multiple aides and cronies. General Motors and Chrysler would file for bankruptcy in a few years; the municipal government in Detroit would do the same a few years later and was in obvious fiscal distress throughout the time Charlton was building Asterand. The city's streetlights deteriorated to the point where some nights, a third of them weren't working, leaving large portions of Detroit in the dark. The city's credit rating had tanked; the property tax base had eroded to only about a tenth of its 1950s' level; residents continued to stream to the exits, moving mostly to nearby suburban communities. Out-of-town photographers flocked to the city's distressed neighborhoods to shoot what locals came to call "ruin porn"— glossy photographs of the city's decaying buildings and infrastructure that captured in computer enhanced intensity every crumbling bit of plaster and pipe. Detroit bled from a thousand wounds, and the city stood as the international symbol of urban decay.

Against this backdrop, the emergence of Randal Charlton's feisty little start-up, Asterand, provided one of the signs of encouragement that a once-mighty urban economy was struggling to be reborn.

A true entrepreneur learns not only to spot opportunities where others miss them, but to act on them immediately. One of Charlton's biggest deals was with his landlord, the Karmanos Cancer Institute. Charlton learned that back in 1979, Wayne State University researchers and physicians had started a breast cancer study. And Wayne State had this bank of biopsy tissue samples that had been used by researchers since 1979. Over time, it had become completely disorganized. The samples were all over the campus, in various refrigerators where researchers had taken samples for their own study and perhaps forgotten to give them back. Some of the fridges were close to breaking down; they were twenty years old, and nobody knew what to do with the samples. Learning of this, Charlton went in to see the interim director, Gloria Heppner, and said, "Look, why don't we take responsibility for collecting them from all over the campus, organizing them, retesting them to make sure they're still good, collecting the data, and then we'll sell them and we'll split the proceeds fifty-fifty." He found Heppner an unusual academic in that she made decisions quickly; they closed a deal in twenty minutes. Charlton went upstairs to his office and wrote up a one-page agreement and they signed it. And then they went to work. Over the next year, Charlton's team organized the material. Then another's misfortune turned to Charlton's advantage: Rice University in Houston, Texas, had their pathology department's bio-tissue samples stored in a basement, and the basement flooded and all the samples were ruined. Rice was deep into breast cancer research and desperate for a new supply of tissue samples. Charlton brokered a deal, and he sold Wayne State's samples to Rice for $4.3 million. Once expenses were taken off, Asterand and the Karmanos Cancer Institute each got $1.8 million. For Charlton, it was more than a windfall; it also demonstrated to his host university that he was someone to take seriously. "It demonstrated to everybody within the university system it wasn't a bad idea to collaborate with these entrepreneurial types who didn't think like academics," Charlton said later. Entrepreneurs, he would say, don't care so much about the titles, perks, and rituals of academia; they just want the best deal they can get by Friday afternoon.

The camaraderie that so delighted Kim Reed and other early employees remained even as the company grew. The first summer, as large numbers of tissue samples began to arrive at Karmanos from around the world and had to be cataloged quickly, Charlton asked his staffers to work weekends. Nobody ever complained. "When you think about the nicest time of year in Michigan, it's the summer. People live for weekends," Reed said. "We worked that whole summer for free. No one complained about not getting overtime or anything like that." At the very beginning, when Charlton had first hired her, the organization was so new that no payroll system had been created yet. "I had been working for him a month without getting paid," Reed said. "It was a new adventure for all of us and we were so excited. My husband had mentioned, 'You haven't gotten a check yet.' I remember at lunch the next day I asked [the office manager] and she looked at me and, 'Yeah, I felt awkward asking.'" Reed sheepishly went to Charlton and said, "I don't mean to bother you, but we haven't been paid. He was 'Oh dear!' He turned red. And he kept apologizing the rest of the day."

Alan Walton, the backer at Oxford Venture Partners, later would give Charlton all the credit for the company's growth. "I'm not sure I'm the person to judge Charlton as a businessman," he said. "But he is the sort of person that 90 percent of people instantly like, and that's a very useful property when you're running a company or trying to do a deal or run a business. So I was actually impressed that in the early years of Asterand, he was able to oversee both the operations and the finances of the company with relatively little background. He learned very quickly. As I said, he's somebody even if he did something wrong, which I don't remember him doing, and you wanted to smack his hands, you couldn't because he was such a nice guy. He hasn't come through the traditional MBA route; he's learned on the job and I think he's a very fast learner and a super nice guy."

Another early hire was Vici Blanc, who had earned her PhD in biology from the University of Michigan in 2000. She had studied genomic and molecular evolution. Charlton hired her in 2002. She started out as a scientific liaison, sort of an interpreter between the sales team and the lab for Asterand. "It was kind of fun," she said later. "Our offices were labs that were converted to offices, jury-rigged for offices. They were set up for people to do experiments, but we used them as desks. And Charlton, the CEO, was sitting right next to any of the employees, sort of dogging it with us in the slums, right? He's a very sort of self-effacing kind of guy. He just wants to get the work done. He's not so concerned about position and title and all that. We worked very closely with Charlton. He was always a resource. He would drive us toward his vision of what he wanted the company to be, give us guidance on how to get there, always with the endgame in mind."

One thing Charlton drove home was trying to get things done without spending a fortune. "He definitely encouraged that. It was an ethos in the company," Blanc said. "He knows where the money comes from in a company. He had to get sales so he's always pushing for sales and rooting for sales and getting salespeople on the team and trying to conserve cash so that you always have some to fall back on." The hard lessons from the wilderness years were paying off in Detroit.

Very early on, Asterand was recognized by Michigan Governor Jennifer Granholm, who gave the firm an award for successful technology transfer and collaboration with the university. That was important because it was third-party validation that encouraged investors beyond Oxford to take a look at them. And it validated Charlton's belief that university research should be put back into the local economy by partnering with small companies.

Over time, Asterand went from occupying one laboratory at the Karmanos Cancer Center to five. Eventually Karmanos needed to take back the space as its researchers began to arrive, so Charlton had to find a new home for Asterand. The City of Kalamazoo offered Charlton facilities and he went over and looked at the business incubator that Kalamazoo was building. "I thought there was only one thing wrong with it," Charlton said later, "and that was that it was way off on its own. The value of the business incubator to me is they put you cheek by jowl with scientists and others who can be helpful to you." So he kept looking. One day, a man named Howard Bell offered space. He was responsible for rehabbing a former General Motors automotive building from the early twentieth century just off Wayne State's campus in the Midtown district of Detroit, on the edge of the university, cultural, and hospital center of the city. He called Charlton one morning and asked if he would come over and talk to a group of architects who were working on the project. The building itself dated to the 1920s and had been designed by Detroit's famous industrial architect, Albert Kahn. It had rich history; the legendary Corvette was first designed there, but now it was surplus property. Bell told him, "I've read in *Crain's* [*Crain's Detroit Business*] that you were thinking of moving, so tell these architects what it would take to make you stay" as part of Wayne State's family. When Charlton got to the meeting with Bell and the architects, there were about seventeen or eighteen people all sitting around the table. Charlton told them at a high level what it would take—that it had to be first-rate lab space but also, since this would be a commercial enterprise, Asterand would need a mixture of labs and office space and also what Charlton called "a lab with a difference." "This is not a research lab, this is a production line lab," he told them. "Think of it as a production line for a car factory, where stuff comes in and goes around, and, in this case, would be subjected to examination and verification and extraction of RNA and so on." And there were extras needed; Charlton asked for a videoconference link so his team could talk with their international partners. Eventually, Bell said okay, and TechTown built it out for Asterand just as Charlton had requested. It cost the university an extra $600,000 to build it exactly to his specifications. He agreed to pay a premium on the rent so that the university would recover the extra cost of custom-building it over time. But the real importance to Charlton was to remain close to university scientists so that they could interact with Asterand's staffers. To Charlton, the whole process of tech transfer depends on being near people who are developing the tech. "So we committed to that space," he recalled. "There was a period where it was quite tricky because Karmanos wanted to take over our lab space. So we moved some of our stuff, including myself, into temporary quarters at Henry Ford Health System, which operated a huge hospital complex nearby and which provided some empty space for us. Governor Granholm officially opened our new home in April of 2004, and we moved in for a day, put on white coats for the ceremony, and then moved out again so the construction crews could continue to build it out for us. We finally moved in."

For five straight years, Asterand made *Scientist* magazine's list of best small companies to work for. Charlton himself was nominated multiple times for Ernst & Young's entrepreneur of the year and was a finalist a few times. In 2007, he won the von Heimlich award for innovative medicine. Charlton got to meet Dr. Heimlich, who is best known for promoting a maneuver to prevent choking. Alec Baldwin presented the award. Those awards added to the sense of teamwork and loyalty that flourished at the company.

Along the way, Charlton's team added to the list of diseases for which they could provide tissue samples. Beyond breast, lung, prostate, colon, and other cancers, Asterand came to offer tissue samples for the study of rheumatoid and osteoarthritis, central nervous system disorders, cardiovascular diseases, diabetes, and respiratory ills. And Asterand's range of products grew, too, beyond mere tissue samples. Soon they were offering researchers matching blood serum and plasma samples, cell lines, protein slides, drug toxicity studies, and much more.

It was time to think about going public. Once again, Charlton looked to the low-cost option. Rather than going public on one of the major exchanges in New York, Charlton merged Asterand with a British firm, Pharmagene PLC, that was doing similar work. It allowed the firm to go public on the London Stock Exchange, where filing fees and red tape were more reasonable. The combined operation retained the name Asterand and remained a Detroit-headquartered firm, and Charlton stayed on as CEO.

Asterand went public in January 2006 on the London Stock Exchange with the ticker symbol ATD. And the investors loved it. In 2008, the *Times of London* gave Asterand their award for the best performing small stock of the year. The company was doing $20 million a year in sales to most big drug firms in the world.

Reflecting on the success of Asterand later, Alan Walton put it this way: "Our competitor in Boston I think spent $60 million is the rumor and was going nowhere and went bankrupt. We basically put them out of business because we were doing more business than they were at about a hundredth of the price. So they gave up, which was good because it brought more business our way."

"A few years from now," Charlton said not long after going public, "I would like to be able to claim that we were the world's leading source for tissue and research services. I would like to see us providing services to all the major pharmaceutical companies around the world. I'd like to say that more than three quarters of the top forty drug companies in the world were using our services. I'd like to say we've built a solid financial base to build the company for the long term."

He had come a long way from delivering flowers and phone books for minimum wage.

With Asterand's stock offering behind him and the company growing nicely, Charlton remained with the company until 2007. "The company had been public for a year, and I was coming up on sixty-seven years old," he said later. "As a fledging public company, I felt I'd gone as far as I could with it. It needed somebody else to take it on who was less of an early-stage entrepreneur, maybe somebody with better organizational skills, more of a manager." In 2007, Charlton retired from Asterand.

If he had stopped there, at age sixty-seven, moving back to Britain or taking up golf in Arizona, he still would have notched a solid success in Detroit. He had created a growing company in a new field with several dozen employees. The state's economic development officials were touting Asterand as an exemplar of Michigan's high-tech future.

But Charlton was not made for retirement and he did not leave Detroit. What he would accomplish for his adopted city in the next few years would eclipse in importance all that he had done before.

CHAPTER 10:

ONE START-UP
AT A TIME

E ven after retiring from Asterand, Randal Charlton still had plenty of energy and still wanted to work in a significant way. He'd always been fascinated by the challenge of technology transfer from universities into the marketplace. Indeed, much of his career had been built upon that process. But he had also seen the process break down at various places for any number of reasons. So as he neared retirement from Asterand, he walked across the Wayne State campus to see Irvin Reid, the president of the university. "I'm going to step down from Asterand," he told Reid. "Is there a role you could find for me?" And Reid, eager for someone with Charlton's skills, said, "Well, I'll make you my economic adviser, if you don't mind working within tech transfer. And you can give me advice."

So in 2007, he left Asterand and became a sort of all-purpose economic adviser to the president of Wayne State. The first big test came up almost immediately. The giant pharmaceutical firm Pfizer, which employed more than 2,500 people in Michigan in labs and offices in Ann Arbor and in Kalamazoo, announced it was pulling out of the state entirely to consolidate its operations elsewhere. It was the latest brutal blow to Michigan's economy, already sagging under the burden of numerous auto plant closings. But this hurt more than most because the Pfizer operation wasn't some rusty old car factory from the 1920s; the Pfizer labs were among the best in the nation and the staffers losing their jobs were the sort of science-minded professionals that Michigan was desperately trying to attract. Hearing the news, Charlton immediately cornered Reid and said, "Look, we've got to be proactive here. Wayne State University's got to have a role here, we've got to go over there, we've got to figure out how we can help, we've got to see if there is equipment we can get ahold of that Pfizer doesn't want, we've got to check how many partners of people working at Pfizer are working at Wayne State, we've got to see if we can keep them by offering their partners jobs, we've got to get heavily involved."

Charlton especially wanted Reid personally to jump on the task, which Charlton feared would be taken over by Mary Sue Coleman, then the president of the University of Michigan, which was a neighbor of the Pfizer campus in Ann Arbor. Charlton told Reid that first day he wanted to get out a press release immediately, that very day, announcing that Wayne State was ready to help. "And I remember going around with Irv to various meetings on the campus, to one assistant after the other in the law department, the PR department, and they were all sort of desperately looking at this piece of paper, this press release that was going to go out that evening and trying to wordsmith it. And I said, 'Forget about the wordsmithing, we've got to get this out, the journalists will take care of the wordsmithing,'" Charlton said later. "They were looking at every nuance. . . . An entrepreneur has to have a level of patience to dealing with the academic approach to getting information out."

So Charlton arranged for a Wayne State Day at Pfizer's facility in Ann Arbor. One result was that Pfizer gave Wayne State some valuable lab equipment it was leaving behind, hundreds of thousands of dollars' worth. Charlton also helped some Pfizer staffers who had spouses or significant others at Wayne State find new jobs.

So that was his first task in his new role. But that role very quickly morphed into something else. Charlton was actually returning from one of his visits to Pfizer when he got a call from Reid. Charlton was driving on I-94 between Ann Arbor and Detroit, and Reid said to him, "Howard Bell has just resigned as director of TechTown and I want you to take over as interim." And Charlton said, "Irv, I've been a tenant there and you know how passionate I am about tech transfer and how important it is to the local economy both locally and nationally, but I don't know anything about running a business incubator."

"Never mind," Reid said. "You'll learn, and you're only interim."

And that was Charlton's total interview for what he later called the most satisfying job of his life.

By some accounts, the idea of a business incubation center goes back to the 1950s, when a man named Joseph Mancuso opened the Batavia Industrial Center in a warehouse in the upstate New York community of Batavia. The idea spread slowly. By 1980, there were said to be only a dozen business incubators operating in the United States. Then the idea took off as the old industrial economy imploded and community after community looked for a new economic model. Today there are well over 1,000 incubators in the United States and several thousand worldwide.

Some in the field distinguish between an "incubator" that caters to raw start-ups and an "accelerator" that helps companies that are a little further along grow faster. It's a useful distinction, but in practice, the terms are often used interchangeably.

The incubator concept goes well beyond the for-profit business or technology park that rents space to like-minded firms. In an incubator, the operator offers a range of services that may include mentoring by experts, networking with other entrepreneurs, meet-ups with potential clients, training classes, guidance for marketing and writing business plans and handling personnel, and perhaps access to capital through venture investors. To pay for all this hand-holding for start-ups, an incubator may get funding from philanthropic foundations or corporate donations or it may operate under the wing of a university technology transfer office or some similar arrangement. Rent paid by the start-up firms may also contribute some revenue.

Within an incubator, a start-up entrepreneur may occupy little more than a cubicle among many, or a lab bench alongside other start-ups. The informality and close quarters generate a feeling of shared enterprise. Guest speakers, field trips, and other events enliven the days. Incubators often host "pitch" competitions where start-ups explain their ideas to a panel of judges in the hopes of winning financial support (like the popular TV show *Shark Tank*). In a way, a good entrepreneurial incubator resembles Hollywood's old studio system where actors not only appeared in the studio's movies but were groomed for stardom with classes in acting, singing, dancing, and how to interview, all the while being promoted by the studio.

In Detroit, back in the 1990s, Wayne State and other entities envisioned a Metropolitan Center for High Technology in a classic old building in the Midtown district that once housed the S. S. Kresge Company, the forerunner to Kmart. But this first attempt to create an incubator flopped badly and remained largely empty. Trying again, Wayne State University opened its TechTown incubator in 2004. General Motors had donated a former design studio building in the Midtown district of Detroit, about a mile north of downtown proper and adjacent to Wayne State's campus. The building itself, four stories tall, had a storied past; it was there that GM's famed design chief, Harley Earl, crafted the lines of the first Corvette. But the building had been vacant for a while when GM gave it to Wayne State.

As it happens, this author covered Wayne State's ribbon-cutting for TechTown as a reporter for the *Detroit Free Press*. I remember being decidedly unimpressed. It seemed that GM had dumped one of its many cold, empty surplus buildings on Wayne State and probably taken a nice tax write-off to boot. Perhaps it was the times that engendered that downbeat assessment. Detroit, after all, was still sliding downhill fast at that point.

At any rate, Wayne State hired Howard Bell, a lawyer, engineer, and instructor at Wayne State's business school, as director of TechTown, and the first tenant to move in was Charlton's Asterand. The State of Michigan's Twenty-First Century Jobs Fund—a "fund of funds" that took money from the historic settlement with tobacco companies and put it to use in various ways—gave TechTown $4 million to operate, and Bell also had cash from a parting gift from General Motors to rehab what became "Tech One," the anchor building of what Wayne State hoped might one day become an entire campus of tech start-ups. A few dozen start-up firms gradually signed on for the initial programs; besides Asterand, the first and largest tenant, the roster included a mix of life sciences, homeland security, and engineering start-ups. After a few years, Bell left TechTown to go to work for an educational products company, and Charlton, having retired from Asterand and working as Irvin Reid's economic adviser, agreed to take over as interim director. The thing to remember is, though they are ubiquitous today across the US economy, business incubators remained a novel concept in Detroit, an unproven idea with unproven benefits, when Randal Charlton walked into the lobby of TechTown as director in April 2007.

From the very beginning, he tried to enforce his vision of a safe space for entrepreneurs. That first morning, as he walked into the lobby of TechTown, he met the facilities manager coming out. Charlton asked him where he was headed. The facilities guy said he was going down to the courthouse to file eviction notices on six of the tenants who hadn't paid their rent. "Whoa! Hang on a minute," Charlton said. "It was pure luck that I caught him," he said later. "Partly I was worried about the headlines that I could too easily picture: 'Tech Town kicks out small entrepreneurs,' accompanied by a photograph of six African American tenants before the TV cameras. But beyond the cosmetics of that, I had a vision for TechTown that did not include throwing out entrepreneurs because they can't pay the nominal rent we were charging them."

And that was the start of an approach that Charlton pretty much crystalized from the beginning. It was what he called his Robin Hood philosophy. If a business incubator is a place to nurture entrepreneurs, then it couldn't treat start-up firms like established companies. He thought of it as robbing from the rich and giving to the poor—that is, TechTown would garner support from foundations and banks and the state government and generous donors and use that money to create a community where people would be encouraged to gain enough confidence to take a chance on rebuilding their lives through entrepreneurship. There were some companies in TechTown that Charlton suspected would never make it—the failure rate for new start-ups is pretty high, after all—but they added to the culture that he was trying to create of "You can do it, you can do it yourself." As he put it in one interview, "I was trying to create an entrepreneurial *church* where people could come and get a dose of what it's all about."

It was nobody's fault in Detroit that for the past fifty years, it hadn't been necessary to be an entrepreneur in the city because the giant auto companies had been so dominant. Lifetime employment with good pay and benefits was the rule—for generations of both managerial and working-class families—and nobody had had to think like an entrepreneur. But now that had to change in Detroit, and change fast, too. The auto companies and their old business model were imploding; General Motors and Chrysler would shortly file for their managed bankruptcies. And it was obvious to Charlton that even if GM and Chrysler survived (they did, thanks to government assistance, and they thrive today), the auto companies would never again employ the hundreds of thousands of workers they once did in Detroit. Those days were gone forever.

So, among other things, Charlton instituted a new rule that TechTown wouldn't time-limit the entrepreneurs renting space there, as other incubators typically did. Many incubators give their entrepreneurs a limit of about three years to make it or move out. But Charlton wanted to keep every small start-up there until they absolutely outgrew the place. He wanted to create a *culture* of entrepreneurship in Detroit. His goal was not to disperse people with good entrepreneurial skills; his goal was to keep them together to build an environment of managed risk-taking. "I couldn't emphasize that enough," he said later. "All that was in my thoughts that first morning in the lobby of TechTown as I stopped our building rep from throwing entrepreneurs out on the street."

There is a downside to that idea from an operational point: Charlton had to scramble to find funders pretty quickly to keep the place going. TechTown, after all, was not a real estate play; it wasn't operating as a typical commercial landlord. What Charlton was trying to do was to build a community of people who had an interest in taking their future in their own hands. So the early days were pretty desperate because of the cost of running the building itself. When Charlton arrived, TechTown was still only about 35 percent occupied, but of course he had to heat the whole building, and he needed the usual staff at reception and maintenance and so forth, so the cost of this overhead far exceeded the rents the tenants were paying. "We were losing money every month," he said later.

Since TechTown operated under the auspices of Wayne State University and WSU's president was the board chair, Charlton went back to Reid and laid it out for him. Charlton told him, "We've got to fess up, we've got to go public with our challenge because hiding it isn't going to help." So Reid and Charlton organized a meeting with Mary Kramer, the publisher of *Crain's Detroit Business*, and a story appeared about "Tech Town in Crisis." And they just laid out what the challenge was. They needed to raise more money to build out the space and they needed support to build a team of people who could provide training to tenant entrepreneurs.

At the Kresge Foundation's headquarters in suburban Troy, north of Detroit, President Rip Rapson read the story in *Crain's* with interest. Rapson, having served as deputy mayor in Minneapolis before taking the Kresge Foundation job, nurtured a love of cities and a deep interest in contributing to urban revitalization. And this was about the time that interest had begun to grow in what might take the place of the giant automotive employers. So he called Irvin Reid and set up a meeting with him and Charlton to talk about how Kresge might help the university's promising but cash-short incubator.

Before the meeting, Rapson didn't know much about TechTown, or about Randal Charlton, other than that Charlton had run a biotech firm called Asterand in the TechTown building. Rapson later said he went into the meeting thinking TechTown was about a single company and he left with a whole new vision for how TechTown might contribute to the larger rebirth of Detroit.

"It was this sort of combination of finding what you expected to find and finding something that was really quite extraordinary," Rapson said later. "I mean, at some level I sort of expected a brilliant, idiosyncratic, driven entrepreneur doing stuff that people couldn't imagine. And it was all there. It was wild what he was doing with cell cloning" at Asterand. But Rapson pressed him on what TechTown was all about. Was TechTown about just one business or about something more?

"And then he went into this very elegant description of exactly that, which surprised me because usually entrepreneurs are so self-focused that they can't usually see the larger machine they're trying to create," Rapson said. "And he was very clear about it. And I remember coming back and saying I went in thinking this was about one company. I came out thinking it was a way of reimagining at least a part of the Detroit economy."

Speaking to his staffer Laura Trudeau, who was running Kresge's Detroit office, Rapson told her, "We just can't let this fail."

Kresge came through fairly quickly with about $2 million in help for TechTown, although the process illustrated how the mindsets and ways of operating differed between an entrepreneur and a large organization. When Rapson told Charlton and Reid to put in a request for funding, they did so immediately. But Charlton remained pretty anxious during this time about how to pay TechTown's bills—his years in the wilderness had taught him to watch every penny—and before the Kresge grant came through, he was calling up Laura Trudeau probably more than he should. He had never put in for a grant of this sort and he wasn't quite sure what they wanted from him, so he was anxiously calling her up to work on the proposal, even calling her at home at 9:00 p.m. At one point she said to him, "Randal, you do understand that this isn't normal?" In the world of philanthropy, that wasn't how things were done. She said, "I'm happy to take your call, but please understand that you are being granted every consideration." Charlton may have been relentless to the point of annoying, and he kept trying to get the grant amount enlarged, but eventually, Trudeau convinced him to let the process work. "So we got the $2 million," Charlton said later, a little sheepishly.

The other thing Charlton needed to get TechTown going was another one or two solid anchor tenants besides Asterand. If he was going to bring in a bunch of entrepreneurs who were likely to suffer a significant failure rate, and many who wouldn't be able to pay their rent on time, then for TechTown to become self-sufficient, it needed at least one significant tenant who was well established and able to pay its bills. This is where Henry Ford Health System stepped in. Created decades earlier with funding from auto pioneer Henry Ford, and located in a massive complex just a few blocks north of TechTown in Detroit's New Center district, the hospital system not only was one of southeast Michigan's leading health providers, but a major Detroit employer with thousands of people on their payroll. Charlton met with the CEO, Nancy Schlichting, and one of her top aides, Jim Connolly, and they were both supportive. They agreed to take space at TechTown and, in exchange for an adjustment in their rent, they would provide some of the capital to build out the rest of the building. They provided $3 million dollars for that, and it helped enormously in those early days.

Charlton also wanted TechTown to expand its capabilities as a center of biomedical research, building on what Asterand was doing on the upper floor. So he and Gloria Heppner of Wayne State took their idea to the State of Michigan's health authorities to move the state's children's blood bank into TechTown. This blood bank was and is a remarkable trove of data. Since the 1960s, Michigan has required medical providers to draw a tiny drop of blood from the heel of each newborn infant to test babies for ailments. The list of ailments to test for started with half a dozen but has grown to more than fifty, and several million of these samples were in storage. The possibility of using them for research struck Charlton and Heppner as a contribution to Detroit's biomed research base, something that could draw researchers to from all over the world. It took over a year to move the state bureaucracy to buy into the idea. "I mean, God knows the number of hours we put in. It was no easy thing," Charlton said later. But eventually the state moved its entire collection of blood samples—millions of individual samples—into TechTown, where it became increasingly used for research.

Charlton knew, of course, that you wouldn't find a giant company like Henry Ford Health System or a state-run blood bank in a normal business incubator. But TechTown wasn't going to be a normal business incubator. This was going to be a business incubator that pulled off a neat trick—to somehow become self-sufficient and at the same time stay open to everybody who had an entrepreneurial idea, whether they had any funds or not. It was a tightrope, but it was a tightrope that Charlton was going to walk.

If Charlton was inspiring, as any great team leader must be, he could also be a bit absentminded. Luckily, he hired just the right personal assistant, a retired legal secretary named Kathe Stevens, to keep him on track.

"I fell in love with Randal when he interviewed me," she said later. "The next day I got a phone call from someone who had found Randal's phone on the street. And somehow, by the two of us talking it through, I realized he had called me because I was the last number Randal had dialed. It turned out he lived on the next block from Randal. So I emailed Randal and said I talked to someone who has your phone and I hope he returns it. And Randal wrote back and said, 'My head would fall off if it weren't attached.' And this is to somebody he just interviewed! So I said to myself, 'I like this guy.'"

As Stevens learned, Charlton had no qualms about admitting what he perceived to be his faults: disorganization, losing things, and being in the wrong place at the wrong time.

"I came in expecting to organize his calendar, but it was soon clear to me that he needed complete organization," she said. "I had to constantly remind him to show up for appointments. But it was fun! I loved working with him. Randal had the ability to inspire you. I worked many sixty-hour weeks for Randal, and I didn't mind it at all. I felt like there was something bigger going on. He just made me feel it was bigger than a job. I don't know how to describe it. He inspired loyalty. He inspired trust. You knew he really cared, that he really, really cared."

When Charlton hired Stevens, there were still empty floors at TechTown. "There were very few tenants," she said. "Everybody knew each other because there were so few people in the building. And everybody loved Randal. Then we got our first big funding, and building up to that was just all kinds of work to convince [foundations] to give us this funding. So it was very busy, but then it just exploded. There were eight staff people when I got there, and we were just 35 percent built out, and when I left there were something like twenty-two or twenty-four staffers and the building was full."

Some of Charlton's more befuddled moments became stuff of legend.

"There was the time Randal left a meeting with a coat that belonged to a six-foot-six, 300-pound gentleman because he thought it was his and never noticed it was many sizes too big," Stevens said. "And somebody had to chase him down at the airport and get it back. I would say the most typical thing was the time he came to work and he was very distraught. He was leaving for Israel the next day and he had lost his green card. And so he was, in a Randal way, distraught. I said to him, 'The last time I saw it I photocopied it and gave it to you, and you put it in your wallet. I saw you put it in your wallet.' He said, 'It's not there.' So I said, okay, and we went through several scenarios. And finally, after some time, I said, 'Randal, would you be insulted if I asked you to give me your wallet?' And he handed me his wallet. And I opened up the wallet and zipped the zipper and there in the pocket was the green card, right where I knew it was. I had seen him put it there. That's just Randal. How can you lose your green card in your own wallet?"

Such tales endeared him to the staff.

"He was the most down-to-earth guy," Stevens said. "He bought all his clothes at a thrift store. He didn't want to use his parking space right next to the building. We moved our office seven times in three and a half years to accommodate others in the building. Usually, he was able to rent out space so he would move us somewhere. We were under the stairwell. We were in this little closet. We were in this little office within another office. And we always shared a space. A lot of times he was in meetings so that worked out for me. I think he enjoyed working closely with me. He was not a technologically proficient person. He couldn't do anything on the computer. I checked all his emails. I answered all his emails unless it was something I couldn't answer, and I would wait to talk to him about it. Again, there was that essence about him that made you feel like you couldn't make a mistake, so I quickly felt empowered to accept speaking engagements on his behalf; I made air travel for him. Part of it was getting a sense of TechTown and our goals. I would only do something that would further the interests of TechTown, but he empowered me to do that."

The modesty Charlton had shown at Asterand, using a desk side-by-side with the general staff and not insisting on CEO-style perks, carried over to TechTown. The small parking lot adjacent to the main TechOne building had a prime parking space reserved for the boss; Charlton refused to use it. Instead he always parked in the same general lot his staffers used a block and a half away. A small thing, perhaps, except that it transpired that Charlton, nearing seventy, would need a new hip soon, and walking from the more distant lot entailed some daily discomfort for him. He never made a big deal of it, but his staffers knew. One TechTown employee recalls seeing Charlton limping along from the distant parking lot, in some obvious distress, because he refused to accept a perk almost any other CEO on the planet would have demanded as a right.

And as ebullient as Charlton was, his past trauma never quite left him.

"I remember we were in one of our offices," Stevens said. "It was an office within an office. And all of a sudden he said, 'I hope you don't mind me being a little distracted today. It's the tenth anniversary of my daughter's death.' His daughter had died in late October, around Halloween, and maybe as a result of that, Charlton detested Halloween. Yet at TechTown we used to have these holiday parties and people were walking around in these ghoulish masks, and once, I knew I could tell it was upsetting to him. And yet TechTown had a Halloween party several years in a row and he never tried to say, 'I can't stay.' He would come to the party, and he would participate. Everybody would be sitting around in their costumes, and I knew he was suffering, but I knew he would never want to stop it."

At the same time that Charlton worried over the money, he was trying to start a movement to popularize the whole notion of entrepreneurialism as a key to reinventing Detroit and its economy one new company at a time. And this is where TechTown's First Fridays and other events became important. On the first Friday of each month, Charlton recruited a prominent speaker and invited one and all to come for wine and snacks and the talk. He planned these events both as a recruiting tool to attract new people to TechTown and as motivation for its member entrepreneurs. Those entrepreneurs needed all the encouragement they could get to survive the harsh environment of the start-up world in Detroit, where start-up capital was scarce and where there was little of the ecosystem to support them that one found on the coasts.

So these First Friday events were part of a whole strategy he developed for TechTown to push Detroit in a new direction, to get the word out that Detroiters as individuals could reinvent their lives without reliance on a giant corporation. While some people naively assumed that the auto companies were going to recover as they always had after a recession and soon all would be well again, Charlton knew, as many others did, that this time was different. And indeed, the events of the recession that struck during Charlton's early days at TechTown and the GM and Chrysler bankruptcies bore that out. Just one example of how this was brought home at TechTown was in evidence right across the street, where a famous Cadillac dealership that went back in the same family about three generations was located. When General Motors started abandoning hundreds of dealerships around the nation as part of its restructuring, this one was among the casualties. The shock of that, and the blow to Detroit's pride of these and other cuts, left the city stunned. To Charlton, these drastic cuts emphasized how Detroit needed a new direction in its economy, something that would provide not just jobs and incomes, but hope.

So while some of the people who thronged to the First Friday events came only for the wine and cheese, Charlton still thought the events served an important purpose. They got the word out that TechTown was in the business of helping entrepreneurs and recreating a city.

Providing the kind of services Charlton wanted to offer entrepreneurs—basic training in business, marketing, writing a business plan, researching a market, and developing a product, not to mention the emotional hand-holding that start-up entrepreneurs need—would take a significant level of staffing. When Charlton became director of TechTown, about six people worked for him; when he left some four years later, the staff was up to about thirty, and they offered a range of programs both for member tenants and to people who came to the public training programs. And the membership thrived. From a few dozen member entrepreneurs at first, Charlton built TechTown's roster of start-up firms to 250.

"The concept was to spread the word that visitors are welcome all the time," he told a journalist a few years later. "Now that has a downside. You deal with a lot of people who if you're uncharitable you might call time-wasters. But I regarded it in the context of where we were as a city as being critical. This was 2007, remember."

Building the staff and providing the services took money, a lot of it, so even after the first Kresge grant, Charlton needed to keep raising funds. In early 2008, he went to see Dave Egner, who was on TechTown's board and then served as director of the local Hudson-Webber Foundation. Egner was also heading up the New Economy Initiative (NEI), an effort by ten leading foundations to pool some $100 million to help redirect Detroit's economy away from the old twentieth-century century model. Charlton gave Egner an idea he had been mulling over—to identify a referee who could be independent and help advise the NEI foundations on where and how to give their money; that is, to help them choose which projects out of so many were the most worthwhile. He took Egner to a meeting of the National Association of Business Incubators. He wanted to have him meet the gurus of entrepreneurship, especially the people at the Kauffman Foundation in Kansas City, the leading foundation supporting entrepreneurial work in the United States. In a day of meetings with the Kauffman team, they worked out an agreement where Kauffman would support entrepreneurial programs in Detroit that would be financed through NEI.

So the very next month—May 2008—TechTown had its first large-scale public event with this new sponsorship. Chris Gardner, the author of the popular book, *The Pursuit of Happyness,* came to tell his story of overcoming homelessness and single parenthood to achieve rich business success. Gardner held three separate events for Charlton, packing in hundreds of listeners in Wayne State University's big Community Arts Auditorium. Then Clifton Taulbert, the author of the memoir, *Once Upon a Time When We Were Colored,* did a couple of well-attended talks. Gardner and Taulbert, both African American authors of note, fitted with the theme that Charlton thought was so important, that Detroit must embrace everyone as potential entrepreneurs, no matter what their education or race or gender or class. Not just MBA students could make it as entrepreneurs, but all people who were prepared to have a go might succeed with the right help. So over a three-year period, Charlton put on entrepreneurial events that drew some 8,000 people. Some of these events were one-day affairs and some were training sessions that lasted several days or took place over the course of a couple of weeks or months. The Kauffmann team supplied a lot of support. "That was a really exciting time," Charlton said later, "not least because we were achieving those numbers while Detroit was digging out of its worst economic crash since the Great Depression of the 1930s."

Charlton also got Wayne State's technology transfer office involved. Universities are filled with smart people doing amazing research across many fields, but professors and graduate students tend not to think in economic terms. And entrepreneurs look at a university and don't know where to start. On a massive campus, where do you go? Universities can be very off-putting places. In recent years, many universities in hard-hit industrial states began to pump up their tech-transfer offices; the idea was to make a contribution to their regional economies by getting some of their research out of the lab and into the marketplace. So Charlton got Wayne State to move its tech transfer over to Tech Town. "I said, 'Let's put tech transfer where the entrepreneurs are and they can mingle with each other,'" he said later.

Another idea he had was to take advantage of Detroit's position on the international border with Canada to promote entrepreneurial careers in international trade. Almost nobody knows it, but the federal government has designated the entire city of Detroit as a free trade zone. That meant that individual buildings within the city could be designated as bonded warehouses to which importers could bring in, say, sugar and cocoa, and they didn't pay import duties until they used those imports to sell chocolate. It was cheaper on the front end of the process. "I think there's a clear future for the city based on the premise that Detroit will be the logistics and shipping hub for the whole midsection of the United States and Canada," he said. Charlton would urge people to look at a map to see that the only natural crossing point between upstate New York and Minnesota was at the straits of Detroit. (The city's name comes from the French word for strait, the waterway where the whole Great Lakes system narrows to barely half a mile across.) The crossing at Detroit already boasted the busiest trade corridor in North America between the United States and Canada, the US's biggest trading partner. Moving a vast amount of auto parts and agricultural products back and forth across the border required a huge investment in warehouses, trucks, computers, and other materials to get them where they were going on time. That's the logistics industry.

It already employed a fair number of people in the city, and at TechTown, Charlton preached to whomever would listen that it was one of the ways in which Detroit would rebound. He got a couple of grants to run training programs for would-be logistics entrepreneurs.

And the idea took off. Officials in Wayne County, the county that includes Detroit, began to talk about an aerotropolis concept—the idea that multiple logistics firms could cluster around a major international airport like Detroit Metro Airport in the western suburb of Romulus. With a major airport, plus an easy highway connection to the border crossing between Detroit and the Canadian city of Windsor, Ontario, and good rail access throughout the region, the logistics industry began to grow. Firms like Penske Logistics, the transportation network founded by auto racing legend Roger Penske, would grow to have a quarter-million trucks on the nation's roads, including entire fleets operated for companies like FedEx, operated out of Penske's facilities in suburban Detroit.

Of course, this entrepreneurial ecosystem that Charlton was slowly building little resembled the overheated start-up scene in California's Silicon Valley. The Valley, besides being laser-focused on the digital industry, already featured a deep bench of talent spotters, angel investors, venture capitalists, lawyers specializing in the legal side of start-ups, and many more players in the high-tech start-up scene, all in the business of turning some of the billions available for entrepreneurs into the next "unicorn" firm like Apple or Google. In Detroit, things were different. It was still a wounded city, with thousands of smart people recovering from layoffs and industry implosions. Charlton took as his mission to instill some confidence back into people who felt as low as he himself had not long before.

"Now," Charlton would say, "I thought the chances of having a new Google emerge from TechTown were like the chance of me replacing Richard Gere in a movie. It just wasn't going to happen. But we didn't need to stake our claim on that. It may be the way to go at the University of Michigan, where there are many more resources and you aren't surrounded by a city in crisis. But in Detroit, where so many of our entrepreneurs were rebounding from a first career (often involving a layoff or bankruptcy), we needed to embrace a broader model of success. In a revolution, you need revolutionary tactics. It's not just about encouraging another Steve Jobs or Bill Gates. They'll find their own way. It's about changing the attitudes of the people."

In one-one-one encounters, in classes, and in interviews with journalists, Charlton preached some of his hard-won rules for entrepreneurs. One was to "play to your strengths." You may dream of opening a restaurant, he would tell people, but if you have no background in food preparation, maybe you should think about something else. Analyze your strengths as honestly as you possibly can. Then, too, he took health seriously because he knew entrepreneurs had to stay physically and mentally sharp. Running your own business will be demanding, he would preach. Consider changes in diet, cutting back on alcohol, losing weight. "You can't do the sort of things you did when you were young and believed you were immortal," Charlton would say.

And while entrepreneurs were by definition risk-takers, Charlton urged them to take only intelligent risks. You'll need to invest in your dream, he would say, but you also need to safeguard your savings and your home. "By all means, take risks, but don't bet the house," Charlton advised. "Bet money you can afford to lose."

He wanted his members at TechTown to "keep the endgame in mind." Do you want to create a lasting company that will survive you, he would ask, or do you simply want to have some fun and create a temporary source of income? There's a big difference. Along those lines, know when it's time to quit. Don't get discouraged easily, he would say, but sometimes, the timing is wrong for even the best ideas. But don't let that put you off of trying something else.

Keeping up with technology was important. This didn't mean you needed to turn yourself into a geek. Just be able to hold your own with basic computer functions such as e-mail, Internet searching, and writing and presentation programs.

And, when a start-up begins to grow, hire to "fill the gaps." As Charlton had found from his own experience, he didn't need to be an expert himself to run his businesses, he needed to be able to hire the right people. So when it comes time to staff up your new company, he told start-ups at TechTown, hire to fill the gaps your own knowledge and experience has left open.

The entrepreneurs who came through TechTown in these days were hardly the tech-happy kids seen on the TV show *Silicon Valley*. Many were middle-aged, often well-educated, but all either needed a second chance or at least were eager to try something new. Dozens of them came to populate TechTown during Charlton's tenure, and he moved through the building each day, encouraging them and lining up all the assistance he could for them.

One of these refugees from a previous career was Sri Rao, a former IT worker with General Motors who was nearing fifty when he came to TechTown. When his career terminated at GM, he got a payout, and he used a lot of those funds to develop technology to help homebound seniors. He got the idea for what he called Sense Aide after his mother-in-law suffered a stroke. "It turned our lives upside down," Rao said. "We ran around with all the typical challenges one would face" caring for elderly family members. "I put together a solution that seemed to work for her and began to look at how I might commercialize this."

Rao's solution was a web-based network of sensors that could tell whether his mother-in-law was taking her medication on schedule, visiting the refrigerator for meals, and otherwise keeping to the schedule laid out for her by caregivers. His technology in essence was a sort of Facebook network for a limited number of people—friends, relatives, next-door neighbors, a primary care doctor, the hospital, and so on. They could stay in touch through a smartphone or tablet, logging in to this private network and touching a screen to see if their elderly patient was taking medication on time, getting meals, and so forth—all reported by the sensors that monitored the medicine cabinet, the refrigerator, and other key spots in the home. With digital technology as advanced as it is, it was possible to put sensors almost everywhere a senior citizen touched and keep track of activities. The sensor network allowed caregivers to look in on the patient if the data signals suggested a problem. Most elderly people want to remain in their homes if possible, and Rao's technology was a way to help make that happen. Charlton would say that it was one of dozens of technologies that might be applied to the needs of America's aging population; the potential market loomed large for entrepreneurs serving this group of people.

Then there was a Detroit woman named Sheila McBride, who started a company called Grade Check. Her business idea, like Rao's, came out of her own experience and passion. Her inspiration was a star basketball player for a midwestern university who was never asked to take any exams. His grades were not a problem as long as he was performing for the basketball team. Then he got injured and, of course, exams came along and he was asked to take them. He was actually illiterate, and he ended up attempting suicide in a tenement in Chicago where he set fire to the building and threatened to throw himself off the roof. Fortunately, he was talked down from the ledge and he went back to primary school, where this six-foot-six guy was sitting in a tiny chair with little kids to learn to read and write. McBride, a sort of unofficial godmother to him, decided she was never going to let that happen to her own son. So she set up Grade Check to help young athletes make the grades they needed in order to get a proper scholarship into a university. She had fights with the NCAA, who didn't want to admit they weren't doing their job suitably, and she struggled for a long time, trying to get into the Detroit Public Schools system. Like a lot of budding start-ups, she went down some dead ends and found it quite difficult. But she slowly developed a software program that monitored a young athlete's grades. The program says, in effect, "Okay, you're trying to get into this type of college, you need this, this, this and this. An A in bowling doesn't cut it; you've got to get into English class and get at least a 3.0 average." Her program was designed to help parents, coaches, and schools pay attention and give support to outstanding young athletes.

When Charlton met McBride, he knew she was not a successful businesswoman and that she needed a lot of help with even basic business skills, so he put her company into what he called TechTown's intensive care unit. He had TechTown's financial manager take over her company checkbook, and they mentored and monitored her so she could concentrate on sales and developing her product. And it worked. She did a lot of good and counseled many young athletes about what they need to succeed in college.

Charlton's work with Mame Jackson illustrated his core philosophy about TechTown's mission, which is that Detroit wasn't going to rebound with technology companies alone. "We're rebuilding a city, and we've got to encourage everything from mom-and-pop corner stores to the arts to technology," he would say. "It may be fine in Silicon Valley to focus just on digital technology because they've got everything else there, including the deep bench of talent, the venture capital firms, the whole infrastructure of talent-spotters and pitch events where everyone gathers to do deals. But we have virtually none of that in Detroit, where the decline of the auto industry left a huge gap in the economic and cultural scene."

Jackson came to TechTown after a long career as an art history professor at Wayne State University. She and her business partner, a Dominican nun named Sister Barbara Cervenka, were importing art from Latin American on a nonprofit basis to showcase the richness of a culture that blends African, Incan, Mayan, and other native themes. When she suggested that she and Cervenka operate from space at TechTown, Charlton embraced the chance to have them as residents. He thought it was absolutely critical to have the arts involved because artistic people think differently from scientific people and they very often think in completely out-of-the-box ways. And Jackson was someone pretty special. Her influence in a quiet way was extraordinary. She was reaching out to communities to get graduate students involved with young people in some of Detroit's toughest areas where there was very little hope. "I think she's a real leader, quite honestly a phenomenal resource," Charlton said. "She lists me as an adviser, but she doesn't need any advice from me. I'll give her any help I can."

So Charlton was happy to have Jackson's company, Con Vida (a rough translation of the phrase "with life"), at TechTown. The rent wasn't always paid on time and there was never going to be a big profit from what Con Vida did—the collection of imported artworks eventually would make its way to a museum—but nonetheless, he championed Con Vida as essential to TechTown.

Ramiro Ramirez also reinvented himself through TechTown's "Shifting Gears" program, which was a program designed to help refugees from automotive downsizing find new careers. Ramirez had spent a long career as an electrical engineer and software designer for the Detroit automakers and their vendors. "I took a leap of faith," said Ramirez. "I didn't know much about TechTown, but the program was only $500 for three months. I felt I was too young to be put out to pasture. The counselors helped me look back through my career and find out what excited me most.

"TechTown counselors told me over and over again that small to medium businesses valued the kind of career experience I could bring, that I could leverage these skills in a wide variety of ways," Ramirez said. "It all starts with self-confidence."

He landed a good job doing business development for Link Engineering, a family-owned business. On the side, he mentored young Hispanics, helping them define their career goals and think about becoming entrepreneurs. He was someone who didn't necessarily start his own new company, but nonetheless found a new path with TechTown's help.

Of all the entrepreneurs who thrived at TechTown, probably none captured the spirit of the place more than Carla Walker-Miller. An African American woman, she had attended Tennessee State University, one of the nation's historic Black colleges, and earned her degree in civil engineering. She worked for Westinghouse and later a company called ABB, selling electrical equipment to power companies. Working first in the South, she moved to Detroit in 1990 and sold equipment to utilities like DTE Energy, Michigan's largest electric and gas utility. It seemed a natural step to become an independent distributor running her own business. So in 2000, when she was forty-two, she launched Walker-Miller Energy Services and became one of TechTown's first tenants.

It was a good business for several years. "We were selling anything from the meter on the back of a house to the largest piece of equipment I ever sold, a $6 million transformer," she said. Between 2000 and 2009, she averaged annual revenues of $10 million. Margins were thin, but she felt her firm was on its way to long-term success. Then the 2008 recession struck, and because she was selling equipment to feed industrial growth, she lost all her clients since growth just wasn't happening. "My business collapsed, basically," she said. "There was no building at that time. There was only contraction of the market. So starting 2009, not only my sales collapsed, but even orders that were already in progress were canceled. So I was left with cancellation fees and problems and debt. It took me a couple of years to get back up to zero. When the dust settled, I was $250,000 in debt and no real prospects for growth."

TechTown and Charlton kept her spirits from totally deflating.

"Randal was an amazing guy," she said much later. "Interestingly enough, I call him a stealth champion for diversity even in those days. When I was a small businessman in TechTown, he recommended me for a position on the investment committee of Invest Detroit's First Step Fund." Invest Detroit was one of the local specialized lenders beginning to gain prominence serving the city's entrepreneurs. "Their smallest fund at the time was the First Step fund, designed to help small businesses with the first investment. I was on their investment decision board for several years, and it really gave me insight into how investors look at small companies, a level of insight I never had before."

About that same time, she pivoted her business from selling equipment to a service model, offering energy efficiency evaluations to clients. The state had recently passed legislation requiring utilities to help their customers save money on their energy bills. Walker-Miller began offering energy efficiency services, and the new line soon replaced the old for her. And unlike the low-margin equipment sales line, energy evaluation was a service business where people, not hardware, were the main assets. She won prime contracts with DTE Energy, Detroit Public Lighting Department, and others. By 2017, revenues were more than $24 million.

And although she eventually moved out of TechTown when she outgrew her space there, she didn't forget Charlton.

"Randal pushed the companies to get different experiences and relationships outside of their normal organic relationships," she said. "He was a great guy."

There's a common thread to these stories. Besides their pluck and ingenuity, these entrepreneurs were all middle-aged or older, and many were women and people of color. We tend to think of entrepreneurs as youthful, college-aged people in the mold of Bill Gates and Steve Jobs starting Microsoft and Apple in a dorm room or a garage. But during Charlton's time at TechTown, he became convinced that Detroit had a huge responsibility to help middle-aged and older professionals as well as neglected minorities restart their careers through entrepreneurialism.

The old model of the economy in Detroit was dead or dying—the idea that you signed on with a giant corporation right out of school and worked as a cog in their vast machinery until you retired. Tens of thousands of smart, talented people had followed that route and found that it ended prematurely in a layoff as the US automotive industry imploded in the first decade of this century. These victims of automotive downsizing were smart, talented, experienced, and far too young to stop contributing to society.

So at TechTown, Charlton and his team began to think about ways to help these baby boomers develop new approaches to their lives and work—to help them think about how they could start their own new businesses. And before long, he had some pretty good data to support that approach. A survey of all the people who came through TechTown's various programs showed that at least 40 percent were forty-five years old or older. This was fairly astonishing. "Once again, I saw that Detroit was playing a vanguard role in reinventing the American dream, showing how dropouts and refugees from the corporate world could start anew and reinvent themselves—and our city—one new company at a time," he said. "Detroit was the perfect spot for this because nowhere was the need greater than here."

By 2011 Charlton was consciously steering TechTown in that direction, catering to entrepreneurs of all ages but offering special programs to the boomers who perhaps needed help more than anyone.

Word about what was happening at TechTown began to spread. Charlton's emphasis on the middle-aged and older entrepreneurs who needed to reinvent their lives won him the prestigious $100,000 Purpose Prize in 2011, an award given to older achievers who demonstrate in their lives and work the value of senior ingenuity and passion that betters the world in significant ways. Kathe Stevens was among the TechTown staffers who nominated Charlton for the award without telling him, since they knew he would probably tell them not to do it, and he was astonished to hear he had won.

The awards event was held in the fall of 2011 in Sausalito, California, just north of the Golden Gate Bridge from San Francisco, at Cavallo Point Lodge, a former army base that is now a conference center with magnificent views of the bay. Charlton and Lee traveled there along with some other staffers and spouses (including this author, whose wife, Sheu-

Jane Gallagher, worked with Stevens to prepare Charlton's nomination.) The awards night ceremony was hosted by Jane Pauley, the TV personality, and Sandra Day O'Connor, the retired justice of the US Supreme Court, gave the keynote address. Charlton listened rapt as O'Connor talked about her work developing civics programs for schoolchildren; she had a new smartphone application to help the kids learn about their country and how it's governed. "Listening to her," Charlton said later, "I thought, 'Okay, here *I* am getting a prize and here's a woman at least ten years older than me and a retired Supreme Court justice who is getting involved in teaching kids about how their country is organized and governed with a new smartphone app!' That was an abiding memory of that event for me—that, and the fact that it was so windy that evening that the huge tent in which the awards ceremony was held almost blew away!"

Charlton had won awards in the past, but not like this.

"How can I say what the award meant to me?" he said later. "I've had some recognition in my career in the past, but this was something a little different. In the past it was technical, perhaps an entrepreneur of the year award, or a plaque for running a company that was one of the ten best places to work in the US, and that was all fine. But this felt bigger because it was also about Detroit. It was about what had happened over a four-year period in which there was this flood of people coming to TechTown meetings and programs. Our First Friday events went from twenty or thirty people to 1,000 people at some of them. And I got a sense Detroiters had gotten a bad rap from those who said the city's residents had an entitlement mentality. I thought that was unfair. There was desperation in the city but also a gutsy willingness to try anything. A lot of people turned up at our entrepreneurial meetings or went into our training sessions with no background or training in setting up companies, but they were going to have a go. And it felt to me a bit like a lot of the entrepreneurs you find in Third World countries. They find a space or a business idea and, in no time at all, they're on the street, selling falafel sandwiches or recycling tin or exporting exotic fruit.

"It was a very exciting time. Actually, I didn't think the Purpose Prize was for me as such. I thought it was a prize for a team of people I happened to be the spokesperson for. I was giving voice for what a lot of other people were doing at TechTown, both our member entrepreneurs and our great staff. The prize came to me, but if it had been just one person on my own it wouldn't have happened. It went to the whole team of people at TechTown and, in a way, to all the people of Detroit."

Charlton was surprised, the day after the awards ceremony, a day devoted to panel discussions and networking, to find so few of the people from elsewhere in the United States ever thought of entrepreneurship as an "encore career." The typical second or third career most of the people talked about at the event involved an executive from a big tech company taking up nonprofit work after retirement. The idea really wasn't even coming up that there were millions of middle-aged and older Americans who were not well-paid executives comfortably volunteering their time after a buyout. "*My* people—Detroiters and those like them around the country—badly needed a source of income and, even in middle- or late-middle age, might turn to entrepreneurship,'" Charlton said. So he brought it up in his panel discussions. He tried in an impromptu way to work the idea of entrepreneurship and the importance of teaching it to older adults into each conversation. He coined the phrase "collision networking" to describe his approach at TechTown, bringing together people as varied as Carla Walker-Miller and Mame Jackson in the same room. "I rejected the idea of a bunch of old retired men who have held high posts—one's been a banker, one's run a food store, one's run a factory—meeting in a diner to reminisce. That's crazy," he said later. "What we've now got to do is get older people together with other generations, particularly the very young. Everyone's going to have to learn to speak the same language because they speak different languages out of different cultures; but out of these collisions is going to come better businesses. This is the first time you've had all the generations, five or six at a time, from the 'greatest generation' to boomers, millennial, X, Y, all bringing different backgrounds to the world of business. I believe there's a phenomenal benefit to that. I'm not sure I made any converts to my way of thinking at the conference, there on a beautiful fall day overlooking San Francisco Bay. But I hope at least I opened a few minds."

CHAPTER 11:

THE REGION CATCHES ON

All the time that Charlton was building Asterand, he remained a lonely voice for entrepreneurship in Detroit, and indeed throughout the auto-centric state of Michigan. State officials at the Michigan Economic Development Corporation knew of him and used Charlton in a video promoting the biotechnology future for the state. But that sort of thing wouldn't have stirred much attention beyond the immediate industry. Michigan's start-up culture was just too new to attract much attention—or much respect.

But there was one community where the idea of start-ups was taking root about the same time Charlton came to Detroit. That community was Ann Arbor, a college town about forty-five miles west of Detroit, home to the University of Michigan. Ann Arbor enjoyed one clear advantage of any would-be hub of entrepreneurs—a lot of tech-savvy scientists and engineers. The university's computer science program ranked among the best in the nation, and its various medical specialties did world-class research in fields as diverse as vision and cancer.

But that didn't translate directly into spin-off firms, since many within the university looked askance at the thought of commercializing UM's research, which was often performed with government grants and other nonprofit dollars. Generally, UM's tech transfer office in the nineties was a sleepy operation, seemingly more concerned with not making mistakes than in generating "unicorn" billion-dollar start-ups. So Ann Arbor remained an entrepreneurial haven in embryo, waiting to be born.

But that was slowly changing. Even as Charlton was selecting Detroit for the home of what became Asterand, a midcareer computer exec named Rick Snyder was launching his latest career move. He had earned both an MBA and a law degree at the University of Michigan, and he had worked with what was then Coopers & Lybrand as a tax consultant first and then in mergers and acquisitions. The computer firm Gateway hired him away to be a top executive and, later, chairman and CEO in Sioux Falls, South Dakota. Despite the remote location, Snyder enjoyed the chance to become an entrepreneur; he relished the adrenaline-fueled atmosphere of the computer world in the 1990s. Then, about the time Charlton got the call to become CEO of the biobank in Detroit, Snyder left Gateway to start his own venture capital firm back in Michigan, based in Ann Arbor.

One of his first calls was to a lawyer named Chris Rizik, a partner in the Detroit firm Dickenson Wright. The two had known each other years before as fellow accountants and consultants at what became PricewaterhouseCoopers. But they hadn't spoken in years.

"Fast forward ten years or so," Rizik said later, "call out of the blue, he's going to be leaving Gateway, coming back to Michigan, wants to start a venture fund and he's looking for a law firm to represent him." They met in Detroit's Renaissance Center, the gleaming series of dark-glass towers perched on the shore of the Detroit River across from the Canadian city of Windsor, Ontario. "I knew nothing about venture capital," Rizik said. "Literally the night before, I went into the firm's library and got a book on venture capital so I could at least bluff my way through the meeting." But the two hit it off. Rizik signed on initially for two days a week, and within a few months they were partners.

They opened a California office to service start-ups there but also did about half their deals with Michigan entrepreneurs. Snyder had gotten rich at Gateway and he attracted more investors, so the fund initially was capitalized at about $100 million. That was at a time when the next biggest venture outfit in Michigan had just $20 million. Rizik recalls that they found most of their potential deals within the ranks of UM's research scientists. "There were a ton of pitches that come in from the community, professors, scientists," he said. But given the sluggish attitude of UM's hierarchy toward commercialization, the going proved slow. In their first two or three years, Snyder and Rizik pushed out perhaps five companies from within UM.

"In the oldest days at U-M tech transfer, the way it worked was how much you managed to sweet talk the legal people," Snyder recalled years later. "If they didn't like you, you could have the best business deal in the world, but they had this pile of licensing deals or other deals to do and you'd end up on the bottom of the pile."

So, he said, "I learned to speak university-ese. They were really good people, but we spoke two different languages, and so you had to learn how to translate. If you spoke the right way, then you could move up on the pile."

Snyder, of course, would go on to run successfully for governor of Michigan using the slogan "One Tough Nerd." In mid-2018, this author sat down with Snyder in the governor's office in Lansing. He was a few months away from finishing his second term as Michigan's chief executive. I asked him to recall what sort of network or ecosystem for start-ups he found when he returned to Michigan in the late nineties from running Gateway in South Dakota.

He laughed. "What ecosystem?" he said. There were a few small investment funds looking for start-up deals but there wasn't any sort of network in place. The network, he joked, could sit around the small coffee table in his office.

Snyder founded Avalon Investments Inc., a venture capital company with a $100 million bankroll, and later, another fund, Ardesta LLC, in 2000. Snyder, Rizik, and their partners invested in some twenty start-up companies over several years. But it remained a tough sell for a long time.

There were some like-minded people in or near Ann Arbor working along the same lines. David Brophy, a professor of business at UM, had been training future venture investors for years, although many of his students then took jobs on the East or West Coasts. And there was Ted Doan of Midland, Michigan, the last member of the Dow family to run Dow Chemical who, after stepping down as chairman and CEO in 1971, had pursued his interests in philanthropy and venture capital. Snyder met him at a hotel in Dearborn, just west of Detroit, and outlined his goal of starting a new business accelerator in Ann Arbor.

"I asked him could I get like $50,000 over two or three years," Snyder told me. "And he wrote me a letter back and said, 'I'm doubling the amount because you didn't ask me for enough money.'" The accelerator, Ann Arbor SPARK, went on to become one of the state's important start-up and talent portals and one of several business accelerators that in 2020, as this is written, cater to entrepreneurial start-ups in the state.

Snyder told me he came to believe that Michigan needed five things to fall into place for a true culture of entrepreneurship to emerge.

First, there was technology. In a way, that was the easiest for Michigan. "Historically, we were always good on that," Snyder said, thanks to the demands of the automotive industry.

Second, Michigan needed the kind of people who could run new tech start-ups—not the founding scientists, necessarily, but people to run and grow the business side, the ones who could be the adults in the room, the ones who kept the business moving toward its goals. "If I had a list of magic-wand things, the thing we could use the most would be serial CEOs," he said.

Third, money. Michigan was just then beginning to draw more venture capital, and by the time Snyder was in the waning months of his governorship, the level of venture cash in Michigan was many times larger than it had been in 2000. But the state still lagged behind the volume of venture cash available on the coasts.

Fourth, Snyder told me, Michigan needed a type of human infrastructure that makes the system work—the accountants, attorneys, and others who understand intellectual property deals and who see that a start-up is a different animal from a giant corporation.

"In the early days, the biggest problem was you could get screwed up because there wasn't an attorney to understand how to do a deal," Snyder said.

And finally, Michigan needed a culture of risk-taking. "Because when I first came back, our culture was risk adverse," Snyder said. "I still tell people this—there's a difference between avoiding risk and managing risk. One of the key things we needed to learn was how to manage risk, not avoid risk."

Snyder noted that back in the early years of the twentieth century, when the auto industry first boomed, Michigan's start-up culture then was bigger than Silicon Valley later became. "But we were too successful," he said. "If you look at the people that founded GM, Ford, Kellogg's, all those people were some of the world's greatest innovators and entrepreneurs. But two generations later after they had passed, you had these huge organizations. They became risk-averse. They best thing they had going for them was 'how do I keep this good thing going on my watch and get out before it blows up.' That was a big part of my message in educating people."

As Snyder ran for governor of Michigan in 2010, one of the first changes he made was stylistic. He didn't wear a tie—an unusual sartorial choice for a conservative business and political climate. And the reason went back to when he first returned to Michigan from out west.

"When I came back, the entrepreneurial community asked me to facilitate a session on UM's campus," he said. "There were about a hundred people there. I'd been wearing jeans and cowboy boots out in South Dakota for the last six years and happy with it, but I said I should probably wear a suit because I'm back in Michigan. So I put a suit on, and I got to this thing and I had the tie and the works, and of the hundred people, roughly ninety-seven had suits on. There were two women and a guy in a sweatshirt. At the first break, I said, 'Give me a break! This culture's all mucked up. We look like a bunch of corporate people here and I'm done.' So I took off my tie and said, 'I'm going to start wearing a tie again after everyone stops wearing a tie.'"

It was a small step toward changing a culture.

Getting people to staff the start-ups Snyder and Rizik bankrolled regularly proved frustrating. These start-ups often had just the founding one or two scientists on board; all the other necessary skills—sales, marketing, finance, human resources—all those types of people had to be hired. And, Rizik recalls, trying to convince someone from a traditional company, an automotive executive working at one of the biggest corporations on the planet, to switch to a little five-person start-up—that seemed a ludicrous idea to so many in the Detroit business world.

"Back in 2006, I was on the board of a start-up company where we were looking for a lead engineer," Rizik said. "Knew the perfect guy. He had gone to school with the founder, he was still local, he had all the right skills. And we offered him competitive salary, stock options, all the things you do in a start-up." But as the candidate began to ask his questions, they were all about perks and benefits—his vacation time, which people would report directly to him, all the things appropriate to ask if he were being interviewed for a corporate job. "They were big company questions," Rizik said. "And at the end of the interview, the man said he couldn't make the leap of faith, that he just couldn't take the risk of going to a start-up." The irony was that this particular client worked for one of the major automotive supplier firms, and just two years later, as Detroit fell into the Great Recession, this candidate's corporation filed for bankruptcy. Bankruptcies were happening all over the Detroit business world then (General Motors and Chrysler themselves would file for Chapter 11 before long) and with those corporate failures, the attitudes toward start-ups and entrepreneurs finally began to shift.

"This whole idea that start-ups were risky and big companies weren't, 2008 flipped that on its ear," Rizik said. "And suddenly the perception of risk changed—everything is risky, it's just how do you manage risk.

"And a lot of people who wouldn't have thought of start-ups before thought of start-ups."

———

Everybody in any position of business and political leadership seemed to know about this time—say, 2006 or so, deep into Charlton's tenure at Asterand—that the Michigan economy had to change. But nobody knew quite what to do. The term tossed around wasn't "entrepreneurship" or "start-ups," but "diversification." Michigan had been automotive for so long, so completely, and it had paid off well for many decades; but that era was drawing to a rather frightening end, with plant closings and mass layoffs and an ever-dwindling market share for what used to be called the Big Three—GM, Ford, and Chrysler.

Enter Susan Berresford, then the president of the Ford Foundation in New York City. Her foundation, among the richest in the world in terms of its endowment, faced a looming threat on the legal front. Founded in Detroit in 1936 by Edsel Ford, son of Henry, the foundation had long since decamped to New York City, where even Detroit's substantial wealth seemed minor compared to the fortunes in Gotham. For many years, the Ford Foundation gifted its money to all sorts of lofty goals around the world while all but ignoring its hometown. In the early 2000s, the Michigan Attorney General's office was grumbling about suing the foundation for neglecting its founding mission to support Detroit. Berresford, then in her sixties and nearing the end of her tenure at the foundation, took the hint. She began to look, both for defensive reasons and out of a genuine interest, at what the Ford Foundation could do for Detroit. Fixing the economy seemed to be the obvious answer.

Obvious, that is, in the need, but perhaps not in any specific solution. Berresford sketched out a plan to pump millions of dollars into a new fund that could invigorate Detroit's sagging economy, her only stipulation being that more local Detroit foundations would ante up as well. They did. Pretty soon there was a pot of $100 million, which quickly attained the hopeful if unspecific name New Economy Initiative (NEI).

By that time, even the automotive executives themselves understood that something needed to be done. Allan Gilmour, then a top executive at Ford, also served as chairman of the Community Foundation for Southeast Michigan (CFSEM), the local philanthropic organization that used its dollars to underwrite local efforts in education and social welfare. With Berresford's NEI in the works, one day, Gilmour told Mariam Noland, the executive director of the CFSEM, that she ought to work on it.

Noland was slightly taken aback by the directive. "We're a charity, what the heck are *we* going to do about this? But when your chair says let's do something, you do something," she recalled later.

She started out by talking to Paul Dimond, who served on the foundation's board with Gilmour. A lawyer and former adviser to President Bill Clinton and former Treasury Secretary Robert Rubin, Dimond threw himself into the task, spending the next few months talking with economists he knew around the country. He and Noland and their advisers eventually came up with the idea to work on three things—talent, innovation, and culture change. That was as far as it went for the moment, with no deeper pathway to what "culture change" or "talent development" might mean. There was only the general idea that "people in Michigan understood that they needed to get skills, that they needed to get retrained," Noland said. "It wasn't going to be the same old, same old that your father and your grandfather worked in the auto industry, and you were going to do the same thing and, by the way, you didn't need much skill." But if only preliminary, even putting the words "talent," "innovation," and "culture" on the top line of a white board in a conference room provided a starting point.

Detroit, of course, was late to the game. Everyone knew the hot spots for talent, innovation, and culture—Silicon Valley, Route 128 near Boston, the Research Triangle in North Carolina. But the auto industry had been so dominant in Detroit for so long that few people saw the need to change. "This was in 2006, early 2007," Noland said much later. "*Nobody* is talking about it back then."

So Noland visited with her fellow foundation executives to raise money for whatever it was this new effort would attempt to do. Susan Berresford at the Ford Foundation said she would give Noland $25 million for the economic diversification effort provided she could find another major donor to match that amount. The Kellogg Foundation in Battle Creek, Michigan, agreed to match it. And several more foundations chipped in, so that pretty soon, Noland had pledges totaling $100 million. She conducted a national search and hired John Austin, a nonresident scholar at the Brookings Institution and the elected president of the Michigan School Board, a sort of advisory panel to the state, as the first director. Noland dubbed the effort the New Economy Initiative (NEI), with the explicit goal of revamping Detroit's economy to de-emphasize muscles and start emphasizing brains.

Despite having plenty of money and a good director, the initiative got off to a slow start. "I think we were naïve in that we thought we would do what we normally do with projects, which is bring a lot of economists in, stir the pot, get some ideas going, and then put out a call for proposals," Noland said. "Which in fact we did. What we quickly found was that nobody had any ideas of what to do. So that initial call for proposals was premature."

Rip Rapson, the former deputy mayor of Minneapolis, had taken over as president and CEO of the Kresge Foundation in 2006, and the NEI was in some ways his introduction to many of Detroit's broader economic problems. Kresge, named for the family whose five-and-dime stores evolved into the Kmart retail giant, had one of the wealthiest endowments in local philanthropy and would obviously play a big role in whatever NEI evolved into. But Rapson found himself increasingly frustrated with the effort.

"For the first two years of the New Economy Initiative, it was ideas chasing the money," Rapson said later. "There was no real coherence to it. And I think we made some very early decisions that locked us into a course that wasn't very strategic. It was a little bit of this and a little bit of that and a little bit here and it was all of southeast Michigan, and should we do Ann Arbor and should we do Oakland County. It was here, there, and everywhere, and before we knew it, we were spending money pretty quickly without any sort of gravitational pull toward anything.

"I keep getting more and more frustrated because we're pushing money out the door, it's going all over southeast Michigan. I can't figure for the life of me where this is going."

Rapson has become known among his friends and staffers for his doodling—not just squiggles, but big elaborate sketches that on paper resemble Rube Goldberg contraptions, with boxes and arrows and chutes and ladders and different colors of ink. So he sat down one day and created one of these that he labeled the Detroit Innovation Cluster. "It was the craziest drawing I've ever done at Kresge and I've done some nutty ones," he said later. But it encapsulated a few concepts that later became central to NEI's evolution. It showed a multitude of entrepreneurial programs—dozens of them—and it showed them all networked together. It suggested amounts of money that NEI might give to each. And it emphasized at its heart the city of Detroit. No longer, in Rapson's view, should NEI put its money into vague regional concepts like "workforce." It had to get specific and it had to become more place-based, focusing on Detroit, and even down to specific neighborhoods, where entrepreneurship might take root.

The frustrations and disagreements over NEI's direction came to a head at a meeting of the foundation executives in late 2010. Rapson was there with George "Mac" McCarthy, then a Ford Foundation executive who had been heading up Ford's efforts in Detroit for NEI. "Mac asked for time on the agenda," Rapson said. "He gave the most blistering counterpoint to what we were doing. I have never heard anyone be quite that direct and quite that forceful. And he essentially hung his argument on two things. One, it can't be regionalized. It diffuses the energy. You've got to have a Detroit-centric focus. Two, it has to be based in the entrepreneurial possibilities of inner-city residents. It had to be about entrepreneurship. It had to be about Detroit. And then I walk in my drawing . . . and the one-two combination I think changed forever the trajectory."

To be sure, there were some bruised feelings in the room that day, and they lingered for a while. But the effort began to focus on those things Rapson and McCarthy and others had come to see as the right path—centering the effort on redeveloping Detroit's entrepreneurial base, its ecosystem.

Under Dave Egner, the head of the local Hudson-Webber Foundation who replaced Austin as director of NEI, the effort began to put flesh on the big general themes of talent, innovation, and culture by focusing more directly on the start-up scene in the city. Gradually, everyone came to understand that Detroit and Michigan needed to create, from scratch, an entire ecosystem to support entrepreneurs—that panoply of venture capitalists and angel investors, tech transfer offices in universities, talent spotters, business accelerators that would provide cheap space and programs to nurture entrepreneurs, talent portals to play matchmaker between the researcher with a clever idea, and the business-savvy types who could translate concepts into profitable firms. First under Austin and then under Egner, New Economy Initiative funds began to populate a whole range of activities that built up this ecosystem for start-ups. "We're all in on entrepreneurship," Egner told the media.

The State of Michigan was getting involved, too. Since 2010, the Michigan Economic Development Corporation made it a priority to funnel state capital into several early-stage investment funds to support entrepreneurs. State money totaling $40 million has gone into these investment funds and helped hundreds of start-up firms. These MEDC-backed funds plug the gap between the "friends and family" cash that most start-ups rely on in their early days and the angel and venture capital money available for more mature start-ups. The state's roster of angel and venture capital investors has swelled, too, as the entrepreneurial ecosystem expanded. As of 2020, the Michigan Venture Capital Association reports that 106 Michigan start-ups raised over $73.6 million from investors in the most recent year. Total venture capital under management in Michigan was now $4.3 billion. It marked quite a change from even a decade earlier.

As Chris Rizik said, a start-up culture in Detroit had to wait, perhaps, until the long-suffering General Motors and Chrysler both filed for Chapter 11 bankruptcy. Well into the first years of the twenty-first century, bankruptcy for these lords of Detroit had been an unthinkable turn of events. General Motors—"generous motors" as it was once known, for the largesse it showered on its employees and the community—filing for bankruptcy proved a seismic event for the Detroit psyche.

"The biggest success in changing the culture was when GM went bankrupt," Noland said later. "I think that began the process of people saying, 'You know, the world is going to be different.'"

Perhaps what the stories of the New Economy Initiative and the venture capital efforts of Rick Snyder and Chris Rizik illustrate is just how far ahead Charlton was when he first showed up in the beleaguered Motor City. Years before leaders in business and philanthropy were preaching the value of entrepreneurship, Randal Charlton was living it in Detroit.

CHAPTER 12:
ASSESSING THE PROGRESS

I n one of our many conversations, Charlton urged me to consider how different this thrust toward entrepreneurialism was compared to what happened elsewhere in the world.

Charlton cited the miners' strike in Britain in 1984 and 1985. Britain's coal mines had operated inefficiently for years, and there was little doubt that change was needed. But when Britain's Prime Minister, Margaret Thatcher, acted to break the power of the National Union of Mineworkers and shut down dozens of mines, she didn't take the next necessary step of helping the displaced workers reinvent themselves. Violence broke out on picket lines throughout Britain's coal country. One statistic tells the grim story: the NUM union boasted 170,000 members before the strike; today the remnant has only about 100. Parts of Britain's coal country never recovered from the closure of the coal pits. Those areas remain among the poorest not only in Britain, but it all of Europe.

Michigan, too, and especially Detroit suffered as much economic collapse as Britain's coal country and lost even more jobs. Total employment in Michigan topped out in 2000, and over the following ten years—Michigan's "lost decade"—the state shed jobs for ten years running, an unprecedented losing streak. By the end of the Great Recession, Michigan had lost 800,000 jobs, or about one in every five positions in its workforce. As manufacturing plants closed and bankruptcies rose, the impact on communities throughout the state proved catastrophic, and nowhere more so than in the city of Detroit.

But by 2010 or so, a coalition of the concerned had come forth to do what Thatcher couldn't or wouldn't do—make a concerted, well-funded effort to help the displaced workers reinvent themselves. This took many forms, from Charlton's work at TechTown to the New Economy Initiative.

We must, of course, acknowledge a note of caution. Entrepreneurship and the panoply of workshops and incubators and pitch competitions on display in Detroit would not by themselves solve the problems of mass poverty and joblessness. Even the most ardent supporters of Detroit's entrepreneurial reinvention never claimed that it could. Nor would anyone expect all the start-ups that went through TechTown to thrive; many never got beyond the idea stage. Even in 2020, everyone admits Detroit's recovery is still just beginning.

"We've certainly come a long way. We've got a long way to go," said Benjamin Kennedy, a staffer at the Kresge Foundation who with Rip Rapson, Laura Trudeau, Wendy Lewis Jackson, and other Kresge hands worked so hard on the Detroit programs. "We have to be careful not to overstate the ability of entrepreneurship interventions to be a poverty solution. I spend a lot of time in sub-Saharan Africa. There's a lot of entrepreneurship in some of the poorest countries in the world. You still need the automotive sector, you still need the big employers, lots of different things. You need myriad things to bring about a serious reduction in unemployment rates. Education is essential. Entrepreneurship is a tough, tough career road to hoe. You've got to have connections, access to capital. But we've done a lot."

But if entrepreneurship is not the sole answer to Detroit's problems, the new start-up culture beginning to thrive in the city does promise to accomplish two important goals. First, it creates hope. The stories coming out of TechTown held out the promise that even displaced autoworkers, single mothers, citizens emerging from prison, and people of color in disenfranchised neighborhoods could all improve their lot *by their own efforts*. That was the lesson of TechTown and the movement toward a more nimble, entrepreneurial economy in Detroit. That some people, or even many, might fail at entrepreneurship through lack of capital or bad luck or any of a hundred other reasons wasn't the point. *They could try again.* Everyone could try again. Through the movement fostered by Randal Charlton and eventually many others, Detroit had opened a new route to recovery that hadn't existed before.

And, second, entrepreneurship became a crucial element in what urban planners call "place-making"—the deliberate effort to create lively walkable urban districts in which a diverse population can live, work, and play. TechTown itself became a hub for its Midtown Detroit neighborhood, which saw new investment follow Charlton's success there. Indeed, he envisioned TechTown anchoring a twelve-block district in which new development would slowly fill up the vacant spaces—a vision that is indeed taking shape. And city leaders began to consciously map out districts where small business experts would work with entrepreneurs to fill up some of Detroit's many vacant storefronts. In Detroit districts, like the West Village neighborhood or the Livernois district on the city's northwest city, small walkable neighborhood amenities began to coalesce around the new shops that opened with the help of the many new programs in Detroit's entrepreneurial ecosystem. This effort dovetailed with a national trend toward urban living, especially among millennials, but place-making based on entrepreneurship proved particularly helpful in Detroit. By 2020, hundreds of start-ups and small businesses were enlivening their neighborhoods.

Some twenty years after Randal Charlton launched Asterand in Detroit, the city's entrepreneurial ecosystem had advanced orders of magnitude beyond what he found when he first came to town, the time of which Rick Snyder had quipped, "What ecosystem?"

Today, the New Economy Initiative has renewed its commitment and upped its total contribution to entrepreneurship to about $160 million. NEI and other funds, like JPMorgan Chase's Detroit initiatives, were funding dozens of different programs, from major incubators like TechTown to smaller workshops, training programs, pitch competitions, and much more. There was the Entrepreneurs of Color fund to promote dozens of minority businesses, and the NEIdeas competition to give cash to existing small businesses ("been-ups" as opposed to "start-ups"). The City of Detroit used federal dollars coming its way to create Motor City Match, an innovation that played matchmaker between entrepreneurs who need space for a brick-and-mortar operation and neighborhood landlords who had vacant storefronts to rent, giving cash to both sides. Dozens of new businesses opened under the program in Detroit's neighborhood commercial corridors, helping to enliven residential areas far from the downtown core. And these were just a handful of the programs now available.

Best of all, attitudes had evolved to the point where nobody treated those with start-up dreams as odd or deluded. When I met with Pam Lewis, the current director of the New Economy Initiative, she unfurled a dramatic illustration of Detroit's extensive entrepreneurial ecosystem. Somewhat like Rip Rapson's doodling of years before, this tabletop diagram showed some 230 programs and sites engaged in reinventing Detroit's economy. These were not isolated entities each doing their own thing; a network had emerged, with faint lines crisscrossing and connecting all the many efforts to promote business start-ups. The most connected entities of all were those NEI had helped, especially among the women and people of color who were otherwise the most neglected. And at the center of the diagram, playing the role of hub that Randal Charlton had envisioned for it and had worked so hard to create, was TechTown.

We've already met some of the entrepreneurs who came through Charlton's TechTown. Today, the broader network and ecosystem he helped create has nurtured hundreds of others. There's April Anderson, founder of Good Cakes & Bakes, who went from being a single mother in high school in Detroit and a worker on the assembly line at Chrysler's Jefferson North plant in Detroit to becoming a successful businesswoman. She hardly seemed a candidate for starting her own firm. But she went back to school, earned an MBA from the University of Michigan, worked in Chrysler's financial arm for a time, and then listened to an inner voice that told her she should take a chance on her love of baking. She struggled at first, getting help from her parents and doing it all more or less on her own without paid employees until her bakery started to catch on. But today, she not only runs a profitable bake shop and catering line on Detroit's northwest side, she's been featured at major events, from the Clinton Global Initiative to CityLab, conferences devoted to exploring urban successes.

Then there was Kristen Ussery, cofounder of Detroit Vegan Soul, a vegetarian eatery now with two locations. She, too, took advantage of the many programs available to fledging start-ups, and as a result was able to ride out the early difficult start-up days. Or there is Phil Cooley, who put aside a successful career as a model to cofound Slows Bar BQ, perhaps Detroit's most successful ribs and pulled pork restaurant, celebrated in numerous national publications. All these success stories inspire others.

"Twenty years ago, fifteen years ago, if you were an entrepreneur in this town, it meant you couldn't get a job," Lewis told me. "I think that's gone. We're not waiting for Mark Zuckerberg. We're waiting for all the little Kristen Usserys and all the little April Andersons and all the Phil Cooleys.

"And we ensure that no matter what the zip code is or the gender or the race, that they can tap into resources and capital and a community that's cheering for them and wants them to win and celebrate their success," Lewis told me. "I think we've done good at that."

CHAPTER 13:
LESSONS FROM DETROIT

Few cities have worked as hard to reinvent themselves as Detroit, but then, few needed to. All cities suffered their share of urban ills in mid-to-late twentieth century. None suffered the degree of abandonment and economic collapse that scarred Detroit.

Could it have been otherwise? If Detroit's leaders had addressed their problems early on, could they have staunched the bleeding before it became a hemorrhage? Perhaps, if leaders had heeded what we might call the "lessons from Detroit." Let's consider what a few of those lessons might be.

First, a city must recognize when its trajectory has changed. That was hard for Detroit when, in the 1960s and 1970s, still seemingly at the height of its power and influence, competition from foreign automakers and the new suburbs began to nibble away at the city's wealth. But we now know that putting off tough decisions until the next budget year, the next election, or to somewhere else down the road, as Detroit officialdom did for so many years, leads only to more profound problems. Denial played a huge part in Detroit's half century of misery.

Then, too, cities need to understand that mere tinkering around the edges of problems rarely works. All those Detroit tax increases that shored up the city's budget for a time did little more than put off the big reckoning. The region's refusal to grapple with the legacy of racism continues to impede recovery efforts.

And in the struggle for urban revitalization, we need to remember that leadership comes from many places far from city hall. Even as Detroit's elected officials and its automotive executives proved inept, unwilling, or corrupt, there were countless neighborhood activists, community gardeners, nonprofit leaders, philanthropic donors, and ordinary citizens who played significant roles in Detroit's resurrection.

There's an old bit of wisdom that I like: Nothing works but everything might. It means that there are no silver-bullet solutions to our urban problems, no single thing that by itself will turn around a city. But if we try a hundred different things and each one moves the needle forward even just a fraction, by trying so many things, we may achieve significant progress.

And that may be the chief lesson to take from the death and rebirth of Detroit. The big showcase projects over the years did little good, like the building of the Renaissance Center in the 1970s or, earlier, the sweeping urban renewal projects of the 1950s and 1960s. Indeed, those urban renewal projects, by destroying older but still vital neighborhoods like Black Bottom and much of Corktown, may have hastened the decline of the city.

From about 2000 onward, Detroit learned to attack its numerous problems with more realistic solutions across a multitude of fronts. Whatever the issue—workforce development, blight removal, prisoner reentry, school reform, new management for venues like the city's Eastern Market, and dozens more—Detroit began to apply thoughtful new solutions by combining public and private energy in ways that finally made a difference. As the third decade of this century opened, Detroit still had a long way to go. But, at least in the days before the dreadful COVID-19 pandemic hit, the feeling was inescapable that the city's troubles had bottomed out and better days were ahead. The COVID-19 pandemic set Detroit back in significant ways and took the lives of far too many city residents. But unlike in the previous decades of slow-motion decline, at least by 2020, the skill sets of the city's economic, political, and nonprofit leadership—and of residents themselves—were more attuned to face the difficult road ahead post-COVID.

And among these many efforts, the drive toward a more entrepreneurial economy has proven more successful than anyone had a right to imagine when it started back in 2000. Detroit may still be a big-company town, and the auto industry remains central to the city's identity. But every day, Detroiters hear of another start-up, another homegrown entrepreneur who has defied the odds to build something new. Detroiters like April Anderson and Carla Walker-Miller and all the others we've considered typify a new economy and a new spirit in Detroit. Like the city as a whole, entrepreneurship still has a distance to travel to reach its full potential. But it's on the way.

And the habits of thought and action that Randal Charlton brought to Detroit in 2000 played a key role in that journey. Nimble thinking, a penchant for action, seeing failure not as the end but as part of the process, and, most of all, a belief that entrepreneurship can give hope to the dispossessed—all these created a new way of thinking in a city desperate to rise from the ashes of its old way of life.

Numerous people have played and are playing a role in turning Detroit around. But when future historians write about Detroit's comeback, they ought not neglect the story of the busted British entrepreneur who came to Detroit at a low point in his life and helped reinvent a city's economy.

AFTERWORD

When Randal Charlton retired from TechTown in late 2011, he immediately moved on to his next ventures. Among much else, he resurrected his book project about his father Warwick Charlton's adventures building the *Mayflower II* and sailing it to America in the 1950s; he called his book *The Wicked Pilgrim* (a play on the original Pilgrims and his father's rather unorthodox style) and published it in 2019. And part of his time he devoted to counseling other start-ups. Nearing eighty by 2020, he also serves on the board of the Hannan Foundation, a philanthropic group that runs many programs for the elderly. Charlton is taking some of his $100,000 Purpose Prize money to work up an art competition for amateur artists in their senior years. The idea is based off the Art Prize in Grand Rapids, in which numerous artists place their works around the city, some indoors and many on street corners or in parking lots, with the public voting on the winning entries. Charlton's plans envisage that old age can remain as vital as our younger years, part of what he calls "creative aging."

"In my youth in England," he told me, "when a man got to my age, he usually needed one or two walking sticks and perhaps he had cataracts that clouded his vision. But now, thanks to hip replacements and modern eye surgery, we've added not just years, but many useful, productive years to our lives. Retire? Come on. Talk to me again in five or ten years and I'll probably have a lot more adventures to recount."

Having weathered his wilderness years and gone on to achieve great things in Detroit, Charlton never forgets how close he came to giving in to failure and depression.

"I still need to work on my self-confidence at times," he told me during one of our many conversations. "Once lost, confidence can return, but you have to work on it. The nature of confidence—that belief in one's ability to tackle any task and get a good outcome—that's such a fragile thing. Without confidence, I spun my wheels for several years. With it, I—and you—can do many things, amazing things you may never have dreamed were within you to achieve."

He went on, "Maybe I've always been prepared to make a fool of myself, to not being embarrassed to fail. But that trait, which an entrepreneur needs in great measure, is something I've developed over the years. I'm ready to dive in at the deep end, whether in public speaking or starting a new company."

Detroit, too, had lost its confidence, had sunk into its own wilderness years. But now this long-suffering city is starting to grow again, or at least, while facing still daunting challenges like the COVID-19 pandemic, it's willing to make a go of it, to carry on in the face of adversity. Detroit is willing to *believe* again, believe in itself and its possibilities. Many people contributed to this restoration of Detroit's morale, not least a remarkable Brit who came here at the lowest point in his life and helped himself and this city find a way back.

"I'm not particularly wealthy," Charlton told me once, "certainly not on the level of Bill Gates or anyone remotely like him. *But I've led a content-rich life.*"

Detroit has been the better for it.

NOTES AND ACKNOWLEDGMENTS

The main source material for this book are the conversations between the author and Randal Charlton over a period of several years. But many other people contributed their memories and insights to the story of Detroit's economic turnaround. Among those the author interviewed for this book, are, in alphabetical order: Vici Blanc, Dave Egner, Sheu-Jane Gallagher, Gloria Heppner, Wendy Lewis Jackson, Benjamin Kennedy, Pam Lewis, James Marsh, George "Mac" McCarthy, Mariam Noland, Rip Rapson, Sri Rao, Kim Reed, Chris Rizik, Rick Snyder, Kathe Stevens, Laura Trudeau, Carla Walker-Miller, and Alan Walton.

For more on the damage that urban renewal did to the Black Bottom and Corktown districts, see "When Detroit Paved Over Paradise" in the *Detroit Free Press* on December 15, 2013, and "Here's What You Might Not Know about Corktown's History" in the *Detroit Free Press* on July 9, 2018. Some of this book's material on Detroit's downfall comes from "How Detroit Went Broke," published in the *Detroit Free Press* on September 15, 2013. This book's section on Preston Tucker comes mainly from the memoir *Preston Tucker: The Indomitable Tin Goose,* by Tucker's aide, Charles Pearson. The section on Henry Kaiser comes mainly from the March 1946 *Fortune* magazine article "Adventures of Henry and Joe in Autoland." The Henry Kaiser section in David Halberstam's book *The Reckoning* also proved helpful.

CPSIA information can be obtained
at www.ICGtesting.com
Printed in the USA
FSHW010618250321
79750FS